GROUP

PSYCHOTHERAPY:

EXERCISES

AT HAND

Volume 2

GROUP PSYCHOTHERAPY: EXERCISES AT HAND

Volume 2

Twenty-eight Topics
with
Exercises
for
Self-Esteem
Depression
Behavior
Goals
Insight
and
Medication

Vacir de Souza, LMHC, CAP, CFAE

Cover design and computer graphics by Irina Nezhevleva de Souza. Cover illustration by Frank Cuzan. Interior illustrations by Elena Yushina. Text designs by Vacir de Souza.

Group Psychotherapy: Exercises at Hand—Volume 2

Copyright © 2011 Vacir de Souza, LMHC, CAP, CFAE

All rights reserved. No part of this book may be used or reproduced by any means, graphic, electronic, or mechanical, including photocopying, recording, taping or by any information storage retrieval system without the written permission of the publisher except in the case of brief quotations embodied in critical articles and reviews.

iUniverse books may be ordered through booksellers or by contacting:

iUniverse
1663 Liberty Drive
Bloomington, IN 47403
www.iuniverse.com
1-800-Authors (1-800-288-4677)

Because of the dynamic nature of the Internet, any Web addresses or links contained in this book may have changed since publication and may no longer be valid. The views expressed in this work are solely those of the author and do not necessarily reflect the views of the publisher, and the publisher hereby disclaims any responsibility for them.

Any people depicted in stock imagery provided by Thinkstock are models, and
such images are being used for illustrative purposes only.

Certain stock imagery © Thinkstock.

ISBN: 978-1-4502-7840-9 (pbk)
ISBN: 978-1-4502-7841-6 (ebk)

Printed in the United States of America

iUniverse rev. date: 2/14/11

Developing and organizing a concise and well-written book with topics and exercises to cover all parts of a group psychotherapy process is a challenging task. Vacir de Souza's books, *Group Psychotherapy: Exercises at Hand* Volumes 1–3, are some of the best-organized materials available in the market. The collection contains a great amount of information, including hints, procedures, group session models, and handouts to facilitate the group psychotherapy session process. They provide a reliable guide to conducting group psychotherapy sessions for the professionals working in community mental health centers, hospitals, or private settings.

The purpose of *Group Psychotherapy: Exercises at Hand* is to provide professionals with specific topics specially designed to gradually involve patients in group psychotherapy in a nonthreatening, comfortable, step-by-step process of increasing positive changes in the patients' lives. With this collection, Vacir de Souza has combined his more than fourteen years of experience working with groups by using an eclectic combination of all interventions available. The topics and corresponding exercises have been meticulously created and organized in a logical sequence to facilitate the group leader's efforts and enhance the progress with the patients. Each topic is diverse and contains at least two different exercises to be used in any specific group psychotherapy session. The topics are intended to offer treatment for all kinds of mental illnesses and poly-substance abuse.

George Dumenigo, LCSW
Clinical Social Worker/Outreach Coordinator, Parkinson's disease and
Movement Disorder Center, Department of Neurology,
University of Miami Miller School of Medicine,
Miami, FL 33136

* * *

Group psychotherapy is an effective and popular form of therapeutic intervention in a variety of settings, especially in outpatient treatment. Although there are many effective techniques and exercises for group psychotherapy, very seldom are they presented in an organized collection designed to cover the full spectrum of specific group psychotherapy.

All exercises of *Group Psychotherapy: Exercises at Hand* are written in a clear and professional style so group leaders will have no difficulty applying the exercises in helping others gain a greater understanding of themselves and make positive changes in their lives.

The three volumes of *Group Psychotherapy: Exercises at Hand* cover all parts of the group psychotherapy process. They should be used by clinicians as an adjunct to group psychotherapy. If methodically implemented, the exercises can open emotional doors in a safe and nonthreatening manner for patients struggling to overcome mental illness, eventually allowing them to live more independent lives and have more rewarding experiences. Group members may feel more at ease when using exercises that are structured, which may lead to improved mental health.

I believe Vacir de Souza's set of books, *Group Psychotherapy: Exercises at Hand*, can greatly assist any professional in the mental health field, including those working in outpatient and inpatient treatment programs in mental health centers, hospitals, jails, group homes, shelters, or private settings.

James Harmon Cook, MD, Psychiatry
Clinical Director, Greater Miami Behavioral Health Care Center,
Miami, FL 33166

Contents

Acknowledgments — xiii

Introduction — xv

Treatment Schedule
- Week One — xix
- Week Two — xx
- Week Three — xxi
- Week Four — xxii

Part III: Group Self-Esteem

Topic 1: Discussing Concepts and Principles of Self-Esteem
- Exercise 1: Understanding Self-Esteem — 1
- Exercise 2: Self-Esteem Disturbance — 3

Topic 2: Assessing Level of Self-Esteem
- Exercise 1: Measuring Self-Esteem — 5
- Exercise 2: Negative and Positive Traits — 7
- Exercise 3: Self-Evaluation — 9
- Exercise 4: Self-Esteem Areas — 11
- Exercise 5: Quality Inventory — 13

Topic 3: Exploring Steps to Enhance Level of Self-Esteem
- Exercise 1: Positive Affirmations — 15
- Exercise 2: Positive Self-Concept — 17
- Exercise 3: Personal Boundaries — 19
- Exercise 4: Self-Nurturing — 21
- Exercise 5: Journaling — 23
- Exercise 6: The Steps — 25

Topic 4: Using Self-Exploration to Increase Self-Esteem
- Exercise 1: Positive Inner Messages — 27
- Exercise 2: Positive "I Statements" — 29
- Exercise 3: Favorite Things — 31
- Exercise 4: Personal Hobbies — 33

Topic 5: Exploring Positive Attributes
- Exercise 1: Positive Attributes — 35
- Exercise 2: Positive Traits — 37
- Exercise 3: Special Talents — 39
- Exercise 4: Self-Worth — 41
- Exercise 5: Personal Strengths — 43

Exercise 6: Positive Qualities	45
Exercise 7: Potential to Excel	47

Topic 6: Exploring Self-Accomplishments
Exercise 1: Past Self-Accomplishments	49
Exercise 2: Ongoing Self-Accomplishments	51

Topic 7: Improving Self-Image
Exercise 1: Self-Image Components	53
Exercise 2: Self-Image Improvement	55
Exercise 3: The Five Senses	57
Exercise 4: Family Messages	59
Exercise 5: Hygiene and Grooming	61

Topic 8: Sharing Reminiscences
Exercise 1: First Memories	63
Exercise 2: Family Memories	65
Exercise 3: Sunday Memories	67
Exercise 4: Romantic Memories	69
Exercise 5: Memorable Periods	71
Exercise 6: Highest Point in Life	73

Part IV: Group Depression

Topic 1: Learning About Depression
Exercise 1: Depressive Illness	75
Exercise 2: Depressive Effects	77
Exercise 3: Depressive Impacts	79
Exercise 4: Stages of Depression	81

Topic 2: Identifying Sources of Depression
Exercise 1: Causes of Depression	83
Exercise 2: Factors of Depression	85

Topic 3: Identifying Symptoms of Depression
Exercise 1: Individual Symptoms	87
Exercise 2: Consequences of Depression	89

Topic 4: Developing Coping Mechanisms to Cope with Depression
Exercise 1: Treating Depression	91
Exercise 2: Identifying Strategies	93
Exercise 3: Overcoming Depression	95
Exercise 4: Fighting Depression	97
Exercise 5: Sleeping Disturbance	99

Part V: Group Behavior

Topic 1: Identifying Inappropriate Behaviors
    Exercise 1: Triggers and Behaviors 101
    Exercise 2: Undesirable Behaviors 103
    Exercise 3: Self-Defeating Behaviors 105
    Exercise 4: Self-Sabotaging Behaviors 107
    Exercise 5: Argumentative Behaviors 109
    Exercise 6: Abusive Behaviors 111
    Exercise 7: Defensive Behaviors 113
    Exercise 8: Decompensating Behaviors 115

Topic 2: Working on Inappropriate Behaviors
    Exercise 1: Behaviors and Treatment 117
    Exercise 2: Changing Behaviors 119
    Exercise 3: Coping Behaviors 121

Topic 3: Learning New and Positive Behaviors
    Exercise 1: Effective Disciplining 123
    Exercise 2: Learning to Be Responsible for Behaviors 125
    Exercise 3: Appropriate Behaviors 127
    Exercise 4: Cooperative Behaviors 129
    Exercise 5: Alternative Behaviors 131
    Exercise 6: Positive Role Models 133
    Exercise 7: Daily Care Needs 135

Topic 4: Discussing Progress of Using New Behaviors
    Exercise 1: Supportive Behaviors 137
    Exercise 2: "Learning Is an Endless Process" 139

Part VI: Group Goals

Topic 1: Learning Principles to Goal Setting
    Exercise 1: Concepts of Goals 141
    Exercise 2: Steps to Goal Setting 143
    Exercise 3: Wishes 145
    Exercise 4: Purpose and Direction 147
    Exercise 5: Realistic versus Unrealistic 149

Topic 2: Making Goals to Work on Symptoms
    Exercise 1: Motivating Goals 151
    Exercise 2: Decreasing Symptoms 153
    Exercise 3: Activities and Goals 155

Exercise 4: Instilling Hope	157
Exercise 5: Long-Term and Short-Term Goals	159
Exercise 6: Goal Commitment	161

Topic 3: Monitoring Progress on Goals

Exercise 1: Master Treatment Plan	163
Exercise 2: Obstacles to Goal Attainment	165
Exercise 3: Ongoing Progress	167

Topic 4: Assessing Achievement of Goals

Exercise 1: "Getting Ready for Discharge"	169
Exercise 2: Present and Future Goals	171

Part VII: Group Insight

Topic 1: Understanding How Treatment Can Help

Exercise 1: Treatment Expectations	173
Exercise 2: Self-Responsibility	175
Exercise 3: "I Have Difficulty ..."	177
Exercise 4: Gears and Combined Treatments	179

Topic 2: Increasing Insight of Unconscious Mechanisms

Exercise 1: Defense Mechanisms	181
Exercise 2: Defense Mechanism Resistance	183
Exercise 3: Defense Mechanism Excuses	185
Exercise 4: Defense Mechanism Blaming and Criticizing	187

Topic 3: Improving Happiness

Exercise 1: Concept of Happiness	189
Exercise 2: Searching for Happiness	191
Exercise 3: Recipe for Happiness	193
Exercise 4: Free Elements	195
Exercise 5: Opportunities for Enjoyment	197

Topic 4: Understanding Oneself

Exercise 1: "Who Am I?"	199
Exercise 2: Perception of Oneself	201
Exercise 3: "What Is Going Wrong with Me?"	203
Exercise 4: "Life Is ..."	205
Exercise 5: "Looking Back or Looking Ahead?"	207
Exercise 6: "Getting to Know You"	209
Exercise 7: My Personal Story	211

Part VIII: Group Medication

Topic 1: Discussing Principles of Psychotic Medications
    Exercise 1: Medication and Symptoms   213
    Exercise 2: Medication Supply   215
    Exercise 3: Medication Safety   217

Topic 2: Increasing Knowledge of Psychotic Medications
    Exercise 1: Medication Action   219
    Exercise 2: Medication Benefits   221
    Exercise 3: Medication Side Effects   223
    Exercise 4: Medication Abuse   225
    Exercise 5: Medication and Nutrition   227
    Exercise 6: Stopping Medication   229

Topic 3: Discussing Psychotic Medications Compliance
    Exercise 1: Medication Strategies   231
    Exercise 2: Medication Tracking   233
    Exercise 3: Medication Compliance and Noncompliance   235

Topic 4: Discussing Medications and Other Drugs
    Exercise 1: Alcohol Abuse   237
    Exercise 2: Caffeine Effects   239

Summary   241

References   243

Acknowledgments

This book was created with the purpose of assisting all dedicated mental health professionals in the field of group psychotherapy who are committed to bringing about effective and practical changes in their patients.

Special thanks to James Harmon Cook, MD, Psychiatry; George Dumenigo, LCSW; and to all the staff at the Greater Miami Behavioral Health Care Center for their support and encouragement in my development of this collection of books. Special appreciation to my co-workers for their feedback and support. Thanks to all my patients for the opportunity to work with them in making positive changes in their lives and for helping me to improve my professional ability as a group leader through the use of the exercises in the group psychotherapy sessions. Furthermore, special thanks to my friend and colleague, Jaimee Hinkes Montalvo, LCSW, for her text review, support, feedback, and suggestions.

Introduction

I am a Licensed Mental Health Counselor (LMHC), Certified Addiction Professional (CAP), Certified Forensic Addictions Examiner (CFAE), and a qualified supervisor to registered interns or provisional licensees. My current work takes place in a partial hospitalization program (PHP) at the Greater Miami Behavioral Health Care Center in Miami, Florida. I have more than fourteen years of extensive group therapy experience working with geriatric, chronically ill, and drug and alcohol addicted patients.

When I started working as a psychotherapist providing several group psychotherapy sessions every week, I quickly realized that we did not have an organized collection of topics and exercises designed to cover the full spectrum of problems clinicians must deal with. The topics and exercises were general, and most of the time they needed to be adapted to meet the needs of the patients. Also, some of their contents were limited. I remember how difficult it was to do group psychotherapy without enough material to be explored during a group session. My inspiration to compile and publish a comprehensive list of topics and therapeutic exercises in this collection of books was to share with the dedicated mental health professionals in the field of group psychotherapy all of the successful strategies that I have used with a diverse population of adults of various ages.

Through my experience as a psychotherapist, I have developed and implemented many innovative exercises for various group therapies. I have combined my experience of working with groups into an eclectic combination of all material for group therapies available in the market. My diverse collection of group therapy exercises has been specially organized and designed to help any professional to perform a group psychotherapy session with minimal effort, while employing creative ideas and garnering excellent therapeutic results.

If you are a beginner in this area, there is clearly an abundance of guidance and material in this collection of books to engage you in this challenging field. The material will help you to develop the skills necessary to conduct any kind of group with self-confidence, flexibility, comfort, and an intellectual perspective. For the professional already in the field, the material offers many remarkable innovations, updating and adding to previous ideas new and creative ways of doing group psychotherapy.

The books of *Group Psychotherapy: Exercises at Hand* are a collection of three volumes containing eighty total topics with more than three hundred exercises for all kinds of group psychotherapy. They are designed to follow a treatment schedule based on the same four-week cycle that is commonly adopted by most community mental health centers, each with four one-hour group psychotherapy sessions daily per group, for five days a week. Volume 1 contains twenty-eight topics, volume 2 contains twenty-eight topics, and volume 3 contains twenty-four topics.

Group Psychotherapy: Exercises at Hand Volumes 1–3 gives group leaders a concise and systematic sequence of topics and exercises to gradually implement in their therapeutic processes. The exercises offer flexible, ready-to-use models of real group sessions that will facilitate the work of any group leader doing group psychotherapy. Each group session model provides valuable suggestions for group interactions, therapeutic interventions, techniques, and treatments. The difficult work of clinical documentation is decreased with these structured exercises. The topics and the exercises may be used in both inpatient and outpatient settings in venues including mental health centers, drug and alcohol treatment centers, residential and day treatment programs, inpatient psychiatric units, geriatric centers, rehabilitation, and chronic care facilities.

This book, volume 2 of the series, contains topics and exercises for working with various kinds of groups.

The group self-esteem section includes exercises about the concept and principles of self-esteem, assessment of one's level of self-esteem, enhancement of one's level of self-esteem, and improvement of self-image. The group depression section contains exercises for psycho-education, specific exercises related to sources, signs, and symptoms of depression, and mechanisms for coping with depression. The group behavior section has exercises to help identify and work on inappropriate behaviors, learning new behaviors, and monitoring one's progress in using new behaviors. The exercises for group goals address principles to goal setting, steps to goal setting, goals for working on symptoms, treatment objectives, and discharge planning. The group insight section includes exercises about benefits of treatment, unconscious mechanisms, happiness improvement, and understanding of self. The group medication management exercises discuss principles, knowledge, compliance, and the pros and cons of psychiatric medications and other drugs.

How to Use this Book

Group Psychotherapy: Exercises at Hand Volumes 1–3 provides the group leader with a series of structured exercises and is designed as a practical guide in conducting the group psychotherapy sessions. Although the essence of any group psychotherapy activity is the use of verbal techniques, the exercises include nonverbal activities, described in handouts, to help facilitate the group discussion. A *hints and procedures* section is included in each exercise and provides valuable information, suggestions, and instructions. The hints may induce creativity to the group leader in a way that makes it not only easier to conduct the group activity, but also provides the group leader with an abundance of material to be explored during each group psychotherapy session. The content of each group session model is from real group psychotherapy sessions and contains the sorts of notes that a clinician would be making about their patients

The three volumes of this collection should be used together for the complete treatment schedule program cycle of four weeks. The topics and the exercises in each volume were designed to follow a treatment program schedule of four groups of psychotherapy sessions daily. However, it is possible to extend the schedule to include more groups of psychotherapy daily within each of the three volumes, because for each topic, the group leader has at least two exercise options available.

All topics have numbers that follow the treatment schedule. These numbers correspond to a specific week (e.g., week one, two, three, or four) and to specific days of the week. The group leader should use the topics in a numerical sequence in accordance with the treatment schedule provided with this book. Some exercises contain key answers, keywords, or statements at the bottom of the page. I would suggest covering them up to hide them before making copies to give to the patients. Finally, I would suggest choosing the exercises used for each topic in a numerical sequence in order to support the development of better group psychotherapy dynamics and process.

Special Note to Part VIII: Group Medication

This book, Part VIII, focuses on educating the patients in a group session on all aspects of proper medication management, including side effects, compliance, supply, and dose requirements. This knowledge is an integral part of the treatment program.

The group environment, properly structured, can reinforce the patient's necessary understanding of medication management.

The educational sessions in this part of the book must be led by trained registered nurses, psychiatrists, or medical doctors. For this reason, the descriptions of the model sessions have been changed from clinician to nurse.

A Few Words about Group Psychotherapy

In his 1985 book, Gerald Corey provides valuable information regarding the nature and focus of group psychotherapy when he says, "Group psychotherapy is a process of reeducation that includes both conscious and unconscious awareness and both the present and the past." In most outpatient settings, such as mental health centers, the main focus of group psychotherapy is in prevention. Most of the patients come to these centers with a moderate to severe level of mental illness requiring a less intensive than inpatient treatment modality to prevent further exacerbation of symptoms or hospitalization.

In general, a treatment model includes several types of group therapies. In volume 1, the model includes group psychotherapy and mental health. The group psychotherapy section is designed to help patients learn how to ventilate feelings, replace negative and irrational thoughts with positive ones, explore their potential for change, and develop independence. In volume 2 of this book, discusses self-esteem, depression, behavior, goals, insight, and medication management. The group behavioral modification section is designed to change maladaptive behaviors. Finally, in volume 3, patients learn coping skills, stress management skills, anger management skills, communication skills, and relapse prevention skills.

Benefits of Using this Book

The topics and the exercises of *Group Psychotherapy: Exercises at Hand* Volumes 1–3 are the most popular and innovative that many clinicians prefer and use in outpatient as well as in inpatient settings. They have been developed to cover all kinds of group psychotherapy and have been organized in order to facilitate the work of the group leader with minimal effort required. Detailed written topics and exercises can benefit not only the patient, therapist, treatment team, and treatment setting, but also the psychotherapy profession overall.

Another important benefit of using this book is that the topics and exercises herein provide the group leader with high standards for documentation. The group session models provided contain the following five basic criteria as guidance for the patient documentation and records:

1. The patient's conditions that support treatment services, such as the severity of the patient's impaired level of functioning and psychiatric symptoms.
2. The patient's observed symptoms at the time of treatment.
3. The therapeutic interventions provided to eliminate or alleviate the patient's symptoms.
4. The patient's response or reaction to the therapeutic interventions.
5. The patient's symptoms or problems that need improvement.

All clinicians must ensure the appropriate documentation of delivery of psychiatric and psychological services. Today, the quality and content of the clinical record may well determine whether treatment is deemed appropriate and the level of care received by the patient is justified. The determination of whether the treatment is justified may be based solely on what is written and, in some instances, on what is not written in the clinical record. The quality of care for the patient is the most powerful argument in favor of maintaining a high quality of documentation. The quality of documentation is an essential tool in the treatment workplace. It is vital to any mental health facility's need for stringent accountability. The documentation should detail what the patient was like initially, what happened during treatment, and what the patient is like after. It should reflect what was done and what remains to be done.

My experience has taught me that learning the skills of effective documentation can be a tedious and difficult process for many clinicians. It is more stressful to try developing this expertise when under the pressure of increased patient load and short time frames placed on clinicians today by most mental health care systems. The documentation demands can be overwhelming when we must move quickly from writing progress notes or other clinical records to other work. *Group Psychotherapy: Exercises at Hand* Volumes 1–3 was developed as a tool to aid clinicians in writing progress notes in an efficient manner that are clear, specific, and individualized. The clinician benefits from clear documentation of the services provided because the topics and the exercises provide a measure of added protection from possible patient litigation.

The psychotherapy profession stands to benefit from the use of more precise, clear, creative, and organized topics and exercises to produce successful changes in the patients involved with mental health treatment.

If you create psychological documents, such as weekly reviews from master treatment plans and daily progress notes, then *Group Psychotherapy: Exercises at Hand* Volumes 1–3 can make your work easier while at the same time assisting you in improving your writing skills. The exercises are designed to help you in writing inventive, tailor-made, and refreshing clinical reports.

A Word of Caution

When you use any of the exercises in this book, including words, phrases, descriptions, sentences, or procedures described in the exercises, you must assume full responsibility for all the consequences implied as related to clinical, legal, and ethical issues. It is critical to remember that effective use of the exercises from *Group Psychotherapy: Exercises at Hand* Volumes 1–3 should not be mass-reproduced for every single group psychotherapy session. They should be used as a guide to help organize the clinician's thoughts, but the exercises should be tailored to account for the clinician's own style, clinical terminology, and the characteristics of any specific group psychotherapy session, as well as individualized for each patient.

Treatment Schedule
Week 1

Time	Monday	Tuesday	Wednesday	Thursday	Friday
8:50 a.m. to 9:50 a.m.	**Psychotherapy:** Topic 1: Developing Group Cohesion	**Psychotherapy:** Topic 2: Identifying Needs	**Psychotherapy:** Topic 3: Developing Positive Expectations	**Psychotherapy:** Topic 4: Encouraging Positive Changes	**Psychotherapy:** Topic 5: Exploring Potentials
9:55 a.m. to 10:55 a.m.	**Mental Health:** Topic 1: Discussing Principles of Mental Illness	**Stress Management:** Topic 1: Understanding Stress	**Behavior:** Topic 1: Identifying Inappropriate Behaviors	**Mental Health:** Topic 2: Understanding Mental Illness	**Insight:** Topic 1: Understanding How Treatment Can Help
11:00 a.m. to 12:00 p.m.	**Self-Esteem:** Topic 1: Discussing Concepts and Principles of Self-Esteem	**Anger Management:** Topic 1: Understanding Anger	**Communication:** Topic 1: Identifying Current Communication Styles	**Self-Esteem:** Topic 2: Assessing Level of Self-Esteem	**Medication:** Topic 1: Discussing Principles of Psychotropic Medications
12:00 p.m. to 1:00 p.m.	Lunch	Lunch	Lunch	Lunch	Lunch
1:00 p.m. to 2:00 p.m.	**Coping Skills:** Topic 1: Developing Decision Making Skills	**Depression:** Topic 1: Learning About Depression	**Goals:** Topic 1: Learning Principles to Goal Setting	**Coping Skills:** Topic 2: Developing Problem Solving Skills	**Relapse:** Topic 1: Understanding Relapse

Treatment Schedule
Week 2

Time	Monday	Tuesday	Wednesday	Thursday	Friday
8:50 a.m. to 9:50 a.m.	**Psychotherapy:** Topic 6: Increasing Motivation	**Psychotherapy:** Topic 7: Processing Daily Life Feelings	**Psychotherapy:** Topic 8: Processing Feelings of Fears	**Psychotherapy:** Topic 9: Processing Feelings of Forgiveness	**Psychotherapy:** Topic 10: Processing Feelings of Frustration
9:55 a.m. to 10:55 a.m.	**Mental Health:** Topic 3: Identifying Causes of Mental Illness	**Stress Management:** Topic 2: Exploring Sources of Stress	**Behavior:** Topic 2: Working on Inappropriate Behaviors	**Mental Health:** Topic 4: Managing Mental Illness	**Insight:** Topic 2: Increasing Insight of Unconscious Mechanisms
11:00 a.m. to 12:00 p.m.	**Self-Esteem:** Topic 3: Exploring Steps to Enhance Level of Self-Esteem	**Anger Management:** Topic 2: Exploring Sources of Anger	**Communication:** Topic 2: Increasing Communication Skills	**Self-Esteem:** Topic 4: Using Self-Exploration to Increase Self-Esteem	**Medication:** Topic 2: Increasing Knowledge of Psychotropic Medications
12:00 p.m. to 1:00 p.m.	Lunch	Lunch	Lunch	Lunch	Lunch
1:00 p.m. to 2:00 p.m.	**Coping Skills:** Topic 3: Developing Conflict Resolution Skills	**Depression:** Topic 2: Identifying Sources of Depression	**Goals:** Topic 2: Making Goals to Work on Symptoms	**Coping Skills:** Topic 4: Developing Time Management Skills	**Relapse:** Topic 2: Identifying Signs and Symptoms of Relapse

Treatment Schedule
Week 3

Time	Monday	Tuesday	Wednesday	Thursday	Friday
8:50 a.m. to 9:50 a.m.	**Psychotherapy:** Topic 11: Processing Feelings of Helplessness and Hopelessness	**Psychotherapy:** Topic 12: Working on Feelings of Trust	**Psychotherapy:** Topic 13: Working on Grief and Loss	**Psychotherapy:** Topic 14: Working on Misconceptions	**Psychotherapy:** Topic 15: Working on Self-Defeating Thoughts
9:55 a.m. to 10:55 a.m.	**Mental Health:** Topic 5: Controlling Mental Illness	**Stress Management:** Topic 3: Working on Stress	**Behavior:** Topic 3: Learning New and Positive Behaviors	**Mental Health:** Topic 6: Dealing with Death Wishes	**Insight:** Topic 3: Improving Happiness
11:00 a.m. to 12:00 p.m.	**Self-Esteem:** Topic 5: Exploring Positive Attributes	**Anger Management:** Topic 3: Discussing Effects of Anger	**Communication:** Topic 3: Increasing Nonverbal Communication Skills	**Self-Esteem:** Topic 6: Exploring Self-Accomplishments	**Medication:** Topic 3: Discussing Psychotropic Medications Compliance
12:00 p.m. to 1:00 p.m.	Lunch	Lunch	Lunch	Lunch	Lunch
1:00 p.m. to 2:00 p.m.	**Coping Skills:** Topic 5: Developing Money Management Skills	**Depression:** Topic 3: Identifying Symptoms of Depression	**Goals:** Topic 3: Monitoring Progress on Goals	**Coping Skills:** Topic 6: Developing Daily Life Skills	**Relapse:** Topic 3: Developing Combined Treatments

Treatment Schedule
Week 4

Time	Monday	Tuesday	Wednesday	Thursday	Friday
8:50 a.m. to 9:50 a.m.	**Psychotherapy:** Topic 16: Working on Thoughts and Feelings	**Psychotherapy:** Topic 17: Working Out Positive Combined Treatments	**Psychotherapy:** Topic 18: Healing Unfinished Business	**Psychotherapy:** Topic 19: Developing Support Systems	**Psychotherapy:** Topic 20: Developing Independence
9:55 a.m. to 10:55 a.m.	**Mental Health:** Topic 7: Dealing with Suicidal Ideations	**Stress Management:** Topic 4: Reviewing Stress Combined Treatments	**Behavior:** Topic 4: Discussing Progress of Using New Behaviors	**Mental Health:** Topic 8: Promoting Mental Health	**Insight:** Topic 4: Understanding Oneself
11:00 a.m. to 12:00 p.m.	**Self-Esteem:** Topic 7: Improving Self-Image	**Anger Management:** Topic 4: Coping with Anger	**Communication:** Topic 4: Increasing Social Interaction Skills	**Self-Esteem:** Topic 8: Sharing Reminiscences	**Medication:** Topic 4: Discussing Medications and Other Drugs
12:00 p.m. to 1:00 p.m.	Lunch	Lunch	Lunch	Lunch	Lunch
1:00 p.m. to 2:00 p.m.	**Coping Skills:** Topic 7: Improving Concentration and Memory	**Depression:** Topic 4: Developing Coping Mechanisms to Cope with Depression	**Goals:** Topic 4: Assessing Achievement of Goals	**Coping Skills:** Topic 8: Reviewing Past and Present Use of Coping Skills	**Relapse:** Topic 4: Improving Reality Orientation

PART III

GROUP SELF-ESTEEM

TOPICS 1–8

WITH

THIRTY-SEVEN EXERCISES

Topic 1: Discussing Concepts and Principles of Self-Esteem

Exercise 1: Understanding Self-Esteem

Purpose:

    A. To define self-esteem.
    B. To discuss concepts of self-esteem.
    C. To become aware of how self-esteem may affect life dimensions.

Hints and Procedures:

Introduce the topic of self-esteem in our modern society by reading and using the information from the handouts. Encourage the members to answer the questions about self-esteem including the following: definition, concepts, and its impact in all life dimensions.

Group Session Model:

The objective of this group session was to prompt the members to share their ideas about self-esteem including the following: definition, concepts, and how self-esteem may affect life dimensions. The group discussion focused on the impact self-esteem may have in the following five life dimensions: social, intellectual, spiritual, physiological, and mental. The peers were to provide and receive feedback to each impact of self-esteem on these life dimensions.

The patient has regularly displayed a depressive mood consistent with his sad facial expression, unkempt appearance, and isolated behaviors. Also, he was constantly mumbling to himself with a speech content indicating paranoid thoughts. However, the patient recognized many impacts of self-esteem in a person's life as discussed by the members. The patient stated, "Nobody wants to go out with me once they know I have psychological problems. That is why I feel lonely and down."

The members added validity to the patient's feelings and concerns. The patient was receptive to the support received and agreed to work on developing an appropriate social support system to decrease feelings of loneliness and raise his level of self-esteem.

The staff will continue to assist the patient to implement strategies to raise his self-esteem level.

Topic 1: Discussing Concepts and Principles of Self-Esteem

Exercise 1: Understanding Self-Esteem

We, in the current modern society, have gained great understanding about how life is, how we should function, and how to be happy or unhappy. The term "self-esteem" is very popular in our society today. Your current level of self-esteem may have a direct impact on your present life. Therefore, it is very important to learn as much as possible about such a phenomenon.

- Some of the questions below may help you to understand what self-esteem is and how self-esteem may affect many of your life dimensions.

    1. What is your definition of self-esteem?[1]
    2. Why do people have a high or a low level of self-esteem?
    3. Which factors can lead to a high or a low level of self-esteem?
    4. Which people are more predisposed to have low levels of self-esteem? Why?
    5. How is self-esteem developed?
    6. How does self-esteem affect one's social life?
    7. How does self-esteem affect one's intellectual life?
    8. How does self-esteem affect one's spiritual life?
    9. How does self-esteem affect one's physiological life?
    10. How does self-esteem affect one's mental life?

---

[1] Possible definition: self-esteem is how we perceive ourselves; it is the values we give ourselves; it is our self-worth or how we feel about ourselves.

Topic 1: Discussing Concepts and Principles of Self-Esteem

Exercise 2: Self-Esteem Disturbances

Purpose:

    A. To discuss the impact of a low self-esteem level on one's life.
    B. To discuss a low versus a high level of self-esteem.

Hints and Procedures:

While the handouts are being distributed, warm up the group discussion by reviewing the negative impact of self-esteem disturbances on a person's life. Continue the group discussion with the questions related to self-esteem disturbances. Encourage each group member to choose one question related to self-esteem disturbances to be discussed.

Group Session Model:

The clinician introduced the topic of self-esteem by reviewing some negative impacts of self-esteem disturbances on a person's life. The members were provided with handouts with several questions related to self-esteem disturbances. The group discussion focused on the content of each question related to the self-esteem disturbances. The members were encouraged to discuss the characteristics of high and low self-esteem levels.

The patient had a sad facial expression, depressed mood, and fair eye contact. The patient was attentive to the group process, requiring limited redirection and prompting from the clinician. The patient stated, "I feel that sometimes it happens in life that you do not know what to do and make the wrong decision. My current financial problem is due to my past wrong decision, and that is why my level of self-esteem is low."

The therapeutic intervention consisted of providing unconditional regard and adding validity to the patient's ideas. The patient was receptive to the therapeutic intervention as well as demonstrated an ability to identify other negative impacts of low self-esteem in people's lives discussed during the session.

The future sessions will focus on assisting and encouraging the patient to explore strategies to raise his level of self-esteem as part of his stabilization process.

Topic 1: Discussing Concepts and Principles of Self-Esteem

Exercise 2: Self-Esteem Disturbances

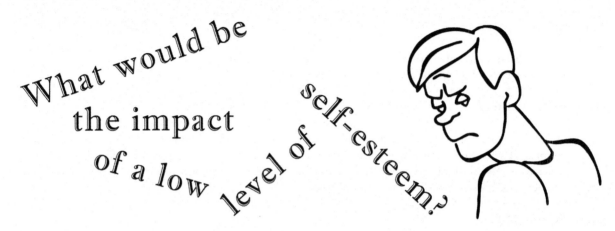

A self-esteem disturbance or low level of self-esteem can have a negative impact on a person's entire life leading to poor coping skills, inappropriate behaviors, self-destructive thoughts, negative feelings, and an exacerbation of mental illness symptoms, among others.

- How is your self-esteem level?

- Now, please tell us:

    1. How do you feel or act when your self-esteem is high?
    2. How do you feel or act when your self-esteem is low?
    3. Which impact can a low self-esteem have on a decision-making process?
    4. Can low self-esteem contribute to an impaired functional level? How?
    5. Can low self-esteem contribute to an increased dependence on others? How?
    6. Can low self-esteem contribute to a lack of self-confidence? How?
    7. Can low self-esteem lead to a lack of personal values? How?
    8. How can low self-esteem lead to self-destructive thoughts?
    9. How can low self-esteem lead to feelings of guilt?
    10. How can low self-esteem lead to an exacerbation of mental illness symptoms?

Topic 2: Assessing Level of Self-Esteem

Exercise 1: Measuring Self-Esteem

Purpose:

    A. To self-evaluate the level of self-esteem.

Hints and Procedures:

Introduce the subject of self-esteem evaluation. Distribute the handouts provided below, and instruct the members on how to use the scale with the numbers. Suggest that the members rate their self-esteem realistically. Nobody should use number zero or numbers too high, such as nine and ten. A score of zero suggests the patient has a very severe depressive mood with the possibility of suicidal thoughts, and in this case, he or she must be hospitalized. Scores of nine and ten suggest the patient has a very high level of self-esteem. In either case, patients should not be in a group psychotherapy session. Each patient should give himself or herself a number followed by a brief comment about why that number is low or high. Also, encourage the members to explore strategies to make their levels higher.

Group Session Model:

The group session aimed at assessing the members' current levels of self-esteem. In order to facilitate the group process, the clinician asked the members to use a scale with scores ranging from zero to ten with the score of ten as the highest level of self-esteem. Also, the members were encouraged to make a brief comment about why the numbers were low or high as well as explore strategies to make their levels higher.

The patient's affect was flat with a depressed mood. He presented to the group session with a low energy level. He was observed as lethargic and fatigued, had diverted eye contact, and required encouragement to engage in the group discussion. The patient commented, "I would say that my self-esteem is at a five. I still feel very depressed, and sometimes, I feel anxious because I do not want to relapse again."

The clinician and the members reviewed the patient's self-evaluation, provided the patient with information, and discussed with him strategies to raise his level of self-esteem. The patient seemed receptive to the group discussion as he demonstrated an ability to grasp the information received.

The professional team has determined that the patient will continue to need treatment in order to implement effective strategies to regain his self-confidence and increase his level of self-esteem.

Topic 2: Assessing Level of Self-Esteem

Exercise 1: Measuring Self-Esteem

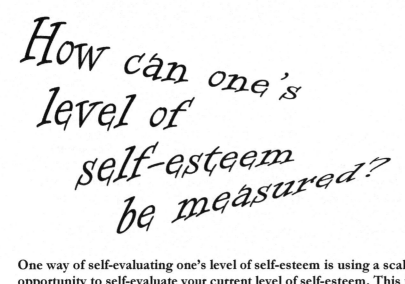

One way of self-evaluating one's level of self-esteem is using a scale. Today, you will have an opportunity to self-evaluate your current level of self-esteem. This is going to be very easy to do. In order to do that, you will use a scale with numbers ranging from zero to ten. A score of zero represents the lowest level of self-esteem, and a score of ten, the highest level. But, please be realistic! You should not use numbers that are too high or too low; otherwise, you would not need to be in this group, and in that case, you should be discharged.

- Please, complete the following:

  ⬥ I will give myself a score of _____ for my current level of self-esteem.

  > Explain why you are giving this score—you should give rational reasons to convince your peers that such a score is appropriate based on your explanation. Remember, you do not need to impress your peers or the psychotherapist; just be honest with yourself!

  ⬥ I am giving myself this score because
  _____

  ⬥ Some possible strategies to raise this score to a higher level are
  1. _____
  2. _____
  3. _____

Topic 2: Assessing Level of Self-Esteem

Exercise 2: Negative and Positive Traits

Purpose:

    A. To identify positive and negative traits.
    B. To use positive traits to raise levels of self-esteem.

Hints and Procedures:

Give a copy of the handouts provided below to the members, and start the group discussion with the definition of traits (see handout footnote). Ask the members to identify their positive and negative personal traits. Encourage the members to use the positive traits to raise their levels of self-esteem.

Group Session Model:

The group session was developed in order to help the members assess their levels of self-esteem by identifying positive and negative traits. At the beginning of the session, the members were asked to come up with a definition of personal traits. In order to facilitate the group discussion, the members were given handouts containing a list of words that described personal traits. The members were encouraged to choose any word that would describe their own personal traits.

The patient appeared disheveled. His mood was initially depressed as evidenced by his downcast eyes and sad affect. His responses were hyper-verbal, lacked association, were exaggerated, and were tangential. In response to the topic discussed, the patient identified one of his personal traits by stating, "The word 'quiet' applies to me. I am a quiet person, and I believe that this is a positive trait, because by being quiet, I do not bother anybody. Also, I can avoid problems."

The members supported the patient's trait, to which the patient was receptive. In addition, the patient was receptive to the group discussion and suggestion to focus on his positive traits to help him raise his level of self-esteem.

The future interventions will focus on continuing to encourage the patient to use positive traits to enhance his level of self-esteem.

Topic 2: Assessing Level of Self-Esteem

Exercise 2: Negative and Positive Traits

What is a personal trait?

There are many ways to raise an individual's level of self-esteem. One way is to learn and focus on personal traits.[1] Personal traits may be negative or positive, depending on the person and circumstance.

- Below, you are going to find some words that can describe personal traits. Try to check off at least three that apply to you.

    ⬥ I am ...

☐ 1. artistic	☐ 13. bad	☐ 25. outgoing	☐ 37. silly
☐ 2. responsible	☐ 14. sick	☐ 26. intelligent	☐ 38. anxious
☐ 3. courageous	☐ 15. ugly	☐ 27. friendly	☐ 39. fearful
☐ 4. creative	☐ 16. overweight	☐ 28. positive	☐ 40. lazy
☐ 5. funny	☐ 17. sad	☐ 29. spiritual	☐ 41. a failure
☐ 6. strong	☐ 18. guilty	☐ 30. generous	☐ 42. negative
☐ 7. beautiful	☐ 19. shy	☐ 31. quiet	☐ 43. angry
☐ 8. kind	☐ 20. worried	☐ 32. comfortable	☐ 44. lonely
☐ 9. pretty	☐ 21. jealous	☐ 33. talented	☐ 45. dull
☐ 10. nice	☐ 22. aggressive	☐ 34. realistic	☐ 46. selfish
☐ 11. serious	☐ 23. stupid	☐ 35. honest	☐ 47. impulsive
☐ 12. athletic	☐ 24. impatient	☐ 36. sincere	☐ 48. intolerant

    ⬥ These words describe my personal traits because _____

    ⬥ I can use the positive traits to raise my level of self-esteem by _____

    ⬥ I can change my negative traits by _____

---

[1] A personal trait may be defined as a characteristic of an individual including ideas and behaviors.

Topic 2: Assessing Level of Self-Esteem

Exercise 3: Self-Evaluation

Purpose:

    A. To identify personal beliefs.
    B. To improve self-esteem by replacing false personal beliefs.

Hints and Procedures:

Introduce the idea of replacing false personal beliefs. While the handouts are being passed out, start asking the members the question, "Can people replace their beliefs?" Continue the group discussion by encouraging the members to do a self-evaluation of their positive personal beliefs and beliefs that should be replaced in order to improve their levels of self-esteem.

Group Session Model:

The group session consisted of encouraging the members to do a self-evaluation of positive personal beliefs and beliefs that should be replaced in order to improve their levels of self-esteem. To facilitate the group discussion, the members were encouraged to use handouts and answer questions about beliefs.

The patient came to the session with a depressed mood as evidenced by his disengagement and isolation, mostly as an observer. However, the patient was able to do his self-evaluation by answering most of the questions from the handout. When prompted to share with the members one of his beliefs that should be changed in order to improve his level of self-esteem, the patient stated, "I need to stop thinking that I am a failure."

The members supported the patient's decision. The patient was challenged to change that belief and others about himself in order to improve his level of self-esteem. The patient was receptive to the encouragement.

The staff will continue to assist the patient with therapeutic approaches aimed at helping the patient to apply the concepts learned during the group task and process.

Topic 2: Assessing Level of Self-Esteem

Exercise 3: Self-Evaluation

My Personal Beliefs

A self-evaluation of personal beliefs can help improve your level of self-esteem. Recognizing beliefs that should be replaced can be a valuable tool to start improving your level of self-esteem.

- Below, there are some questions about personal beliefs. Answer them as completely as you would like to.

    1. What do you believe in? Why?
    2. What are your dreams?
    3. What do you like most about yourself? Why?
    4. What are the values that you like most about yourself? Why?
    5. Where are your sources of hope?
    6. How do you show affection?
    7. How do you show love?
    8. When do you have a sense of humor? Why?
    9. What are your realistic expectations in life?
    10. What do you do to please yourself? How often? How do you do this?

Topic 2: Assessing Level of Self-Esteem

Exercise 4: Self-Esteem Areas

Purpose:

    A. To identify areas of self-esteem that needs improvement.

Hints and Procedures:

While the handouts are being distributed, introduce the subject by explaining to the members that self-esteem enhancement requires the ability to first identify what should be improved. Encourage the members to identify areas that they need to improve. The negative responses from each member should be used to promote the group discussion about ways of strengthening areas that are low in order to raise their levels of self-esteem.

Group Session Model:

The group session was developed in order to help the members identify areas of self-esteem that needed improvement. In order to facilitate the group activity and discussion, the members were asked to use handouts with areas of self-esteem that needed improvement. The group discussion focused on helping each member to find ways of strengthening the areas that were low in order to raise their levels of self-esteem.

The patient was observed as disengaged, mentally distant, and unmotivated to participate. However, as the session progressed, the patient became more involved, and improved on both participation and interaction. The patient focused on his need to improve his social support system. The patient stated, "I have just moved to a new adult living facility and now I have no friends. I feel lonely."

The clinician assisted the patient in finding some ways of strengthening his social support system, such as making new friends at his residential place, attending church, and participating in recreational groups in the community. The patient agreed to focus on the topic in the future and put the ideas into action.

The future sessions will continue to assist and encourage the patient to work on his areas of self-esteem that need improvement.

Topic 2: Assessing Level of Self-Esteem

Exercise 4: Self-Esteem Areas

Identifying areas of self-esteem that need improvement should be an important step toward enhancing your level of self-esteem.

- What are your weaknesses?

- Please identify at least one area below that you need to work on in order to enhance your level of self-esteem.

1. I have no goals.
2. I have not planned for my future.
3. I cannot make decisions easily.
4. I cannot control my impulsive behavior.
5. I do not enjoy activities.
6. I do not like my body.
7. I do not have anybody to talk to.
8. I do not like creating new things.
9. I do not know why I am here in this group.
10. I am not close to my family.
11. I have no friends.
12. I hate being unique.
13. I cannot express my feelings assertively.
14. I cannot recognize that I am mentally ill.
15. I do not like myself.
16. I do not get along well with people.
17. I do not compliment others.
18. I do not know how to cope with my stress.
19. I am not a responsible person.
20. I always expect to have what I want.

✧ One way to work on this area is _____

Topic 2: Assessing Level of Self-Esteem

Exercise 5: Quality Inventory

Purpose:

    A. To identify past and present personal qualities observed by others and by oneself.

Hints and Procedures:

    Distribute the handouts provided below, and introduce the idea of doing a "quality inventory" as a tool to identify personal positive qualities. Encourage and assist the members to complete the quality inventory. Provide the members with support and encourage them to talk about their positive personal qualities as a way to enhance their self-esteem levels.

Group Session Model:

    The objective of the group session was to assist and encourage the members to identify personal qualities observed by others and themselves. In order to facilitate the group activity, the members were encouraged to use handouts with a quality inventory guide consisting of statements to be completed.

    The patient had a depressed mood, was disheveled and unkempt, was responding to internal stimuli, and was constantly mumbling to himself. His speech was indicative of paranoid thoughts and questionable insight. However, the patient described one of his qualities from the quality inventory as follows: "One quality that helps me feel good is that I am a good listener."

    The patient was praised for his quality. The patient was receptive to the praise, but had difficulty answering other questions from the quality inventory and continued to respond to his internal stimuli.

    The future interventions will focus on increasing the patient's ability to participate actively in the group process, so he will be able to grasp the concepts being learned and apply the same toward himself.

Topic 2: Assessing Level of Self-Esteem

Exercise 5: Quality Inventory

Identifying and focusing on personal positive qualities is a valuable way to improve your level of self-esteem. The tool to do that is developing a quality inventory. In this inventory, you can identify and explore your past and present qualities observed by others and yourself.

- Complete the following statements by using a brief description of each quality about you.

    1. Two of my qualities that people have praised and appreciated are
    2. Two qualities that help me survive in life are
    3. Two qualities that help me feel happy are
    4. Two qualities that help me bring happiness to others are
    5. Two qualities that help me reach my life goals are
    6. Two qualities that help me bring love to myself are
    7. One quality that helps me feel good is
    8. One quality that helps me help others is
    9. One quality that helps me learn is
    10. One thing I was good at with my romantic partner was
    11. One thing I was good at with my family was
    12. One thing I was good at my work/school was

Topic 3: Exploring Steps to Enhance Level of Self-Esteem

Exercise 1: Positive Affirmations

Purpose:

A. To increase the use of positive affirmations to raise levels of self-esteem.

Hints and Procedures:

Distribute the handouts provided below, and warm up the group discussion with the definition of positive affirmations. Ask the members whether they have been using positive affirmations and review any positive results from using them. When choosing the positive affirmations, instruct the members to first relax their bodies and then state their positive affirmations aloud while visualizing them as very true. Review the results of the activity and encourage the members to start using the positive affirmations on a daily basis.

Group Session Model:

The objective of this group session was increasing the use of positive affirmations to raise the members' levels of self-esteem. The members chose positive affirmations from a list and read them aloud while visualizing them as very true. Then the members discussed why the affirmations were true. The therapeutic intervention consisted of encouraging the members to start using the positive affirmations daily.

The patient came to the session with his head hung low and poor eye contact. He was generally apathetic during the session. He tended to isolate himself with limited interaction with his peers. However, the patient was able to follow the group task appropriately and made the following comment about one of his positive affirmations: "This is true; I care about others, and this makes me feel good."

Positive feedback was provided by the members regarding the patient's positive affirmation. The patient reacted in a positive way with the therapeutic intervention. He recognized the need of continuing to practice his positive affirmations on a daily basis in order to raise his level of self-esteem.

The future sessions will focus on assisting and encouraging the patient to explore other ways to raise his level of self-esteem.

Topic 3: Exploring Steps to Enhance Level of Self-Esteem

Exercise 1: Positive Affirmations

What are positive affirmations? Positive affirmations are statements about a desired outcome to become a reality. Positive affirmations may convert real thoughts about who we are and what we are capable of achieving. They can help replace negative messages and thoughts into more positive and realistic ways of thinking. They would help enhance your level of self-esteem.

- Please use the following instructions:

    ◆ Choose one positive affirmation below. Relax your body. State your positive affirmation aloud and visualize it as very true.

    ☐ 1. "I am a nice person." ☐ 11. "I am worthy of respect from myself."
    ☐ 2. "I like being the way I am." ☐ 12. "I make a difference in people's lives."
    ☐ 3. "I like my body." ☐ 13. "I am a smart person."
    ☐ 4. "I am capable and competent." ☐ 14. "I am important."
    ☐ 5. "I care about others." ☐ 15. "I am creative."
    ☐ 6. "I can become independent." ☐ 16. "I can keep myself stable."
    ☐ 7. "I can succeed." ☐ 17. "I am friendly."
    ☐ 8. "I am a sincere person" ☐ 18. "I can make people happy."
    ☐ 9. "I can make myself happy." ☐ 19. "I have goals."
    ☐ 10. "I am learning …" ☐ 20. "I will get myself stable."

    ◆ Now, tell us why your positive affirmation is very true.

    ◆ You need to continue stating your positive affirmation daily. Why?

Topic 3: Exploring Steps to Enhance Level of Self-Esteem

Exercise 2: Positive Self-Concept

Purpose:

    A. To promote positive self-enhancing concepts.
    B. To discuss personal self-concepts versus self-esteem.

Hints and Procedures:

Introduce the subject, "positive self-concept versus self-esteem." Distribute the handouts provided below. Promote the group discussion by using the content of each question related to the positive self-concept and self-esteem. Challenge the members to explore ways to improve their self-concepts and raise their levels of self-esteem.

Group Session Model:

The patient needed this group session in order to promote positive self-enhancing concepts and raise his level of self-esteem. The clinician started the group discussion by educating the members about how negative self-concepts can lead to many negative consequences; including low self-worth, low self-esteem, and fears. The focus of the group discussion was on challenging the members to explore strategies to improve their self-concepts.

The patient reported to the session with a mirthless smile, depressive mood, and congruent affect. The patient sat erect with fair eye contact and a sad facial expression. Upon being approached, the patient stated, "I began to have problems when I broke the law and the courts ordered treatment." The patient continued to say, "But now that I am coming to this mental health center, I am becoming more optimistic, since I am learning how to replace many of my irrational thoughts related to my confinement."

Positive social feedback and empathy were provided by the members related to the patient's statements. The patient was receptive to the feedback and agreed to continue working on improving his self-concept with self-disclosure in the group process.

The professional team will continue to assist the patient with the therapeutic interventions aimed at increasing his positive self-concepts and his level of self-esteem.

Topic 3: Exploring Steps to Enhance Level of Self-Esteem

Exercise 2: Positive Self-Concept

Positive Self-Concept versus Self-Esteem

There is a correlation between positive self-concept and self-esteem. A person with a rich repertoire of positive self-concepts has a high level of self-esteem. There are many valuable ways that can help develop a repertoire of positive self-concepts and raise your level of self-esteem. Self-concept depends on the level of aspiration, optimism, interest, and performance on different tasks. Therefore, let's work together to see how they work.

- Please, answer the following questions:

    1. What is a positive self-concept?
    2. Can you identify at least three positive self-concepts?
    3. What are the effects of positive self-concepts on a person's life?
    4. How do positive self-concepts develop?
    5. How can negative self-concepts affect a person's life?[1]
    6. Which factors can contribute to negative self-concepts?
    7. How can aspiration be used to increase positive self-concepts?
    8. How can optimism be used to increase positive self-concepts?
    9. How can interest be used to increase positive self-concepts?
    10. How can performance be used to increase positive self-concepts?

---

[1] A negative self-concept can lead to feelings of fears, low self-esteem, low self-worth, and lack of self-confidence.

Topic 3: Exploring Steps to Enhance Level of Self-Esteem

Exercise 3: Personal Boundaries

Purpose:

A. To raise levels of self-esteem by establishing and maintaining personal boundaries.

Hints and Procedures:

Distribute the handouts provided below, and initiate the group discussion by using the information about the benefits of establishing and maintaining personal boundaries. Continue the group discussion with the remaining questions.

Group Session Model:

The focus of this group session was aimed at educating the members in establishing and maintaining boundaries as a strategy to raise their levels of self-esteem. The clinician provided the members with handouts with information, questions, and guidance about establishing and maintaining boundaries.

The patient was attentive to the group discussion; however, he displayed symptoms suggesting a depressive mental status. He was observed as withdrawn but participated appropriately when directly approached. After some prompting, the patient commented, "I think that self-awareness is a very important step in setting boundaries. People should know where the boundaries are, and sometimes, we need to establish some new boundaries to honor ourselves."

The patient's opinion was well accepted and shared among all members. Also, the patient was in accordance with many other steps in setting boundaries that were discussed during the group discussion.

The staff will continue to assist and encourage the patient to implement the steps to set personal boundaries discussed as an alternative way to enhance his level of self-esteem.

Topic 3: Exploring Steps to Enhance Level of Self-Esteem

Exercise 3: Personal Boundaries

Establishing personal boundaries can make an enormous positive impact on the quality of our lives. They can help us keep people's undesirable actions and behaviors from hurting, distracting, or humiliating us. In addition, they can help us protect our bodies, minds, and spirits, and as a result, they may help us raise our levels of self-esteem.

- Let's learn more about how to establish and maintain personal boundaries.

    1. What are boundaries?[1]
    2. What are the essential steps you can use in setting personal boundaries?[2]
    3. What and where are your personal boundaries?
    4. What can be the unacceptable behaviors and expressions that should not be tolerated?
    5. What do you want people to stop doing or telling you? Why?
    6. What can we do if people continue ignoring our request?
    7. What negative consequences can we set to impact people?
    8. How can we respect other people's personal boundaries?
    9. How can we establish and maintain personal boundaries?
    10. Are your personal boundaries weak or nonexistent? Why?

---

[1] Boundaries are imaginary lines that help us protect ourselves both physically and emotionally.
[2] They may include self-awareness, intolerance, request, consequences, and respect to others.

Topic 3: Exploring Steps to Enhance Level of Self-Esteem

Exercise 4: Self-Nurturing

Purpose:

    A. To strengthen self-esteem by increasing ability for self-nurturing.
    B. To explore components of self-nurturing.

Hints and Procedures:

Provide the members with the handouts. Start the group discussion with the definition of self-nurturing. Use the remaining questions to discuss the components of self-nurturing, its benefits, and its content.

Group Session Model:

The group session was aimed at helping the members strengthen self-esteem by increasing their ability for self-nurturing. The clinician started the group discussion by asking the members for a brief definition of self-nurturing and its impact on our levels of self-esteem. Then the members were encouraged to use handouts with questions about components of self-nurturing, its benefits, and its content. The group discussion that followed focused on the content of each component.

The patient had a blunted affect and dysphoric mood. He was slightly less anxious today, but was observed as being sad, and had fair eye contact and a low energy level. In response to the self-nurturing subject, the patient commented on the component "fun and relaxing things" by stating, "I need to become more involved in fun and relaxing things. I like gardening, and now that I am living with my daughter, I want to help her plant a garden in the back of her house."

The therapeutic intervention consisted of educating the patient about the benefits of self-nurturing and enabling the patient to use the self-nurturing components in his daily life. The patient was receptive to the therapeutic intervention.

The professional team has determined that the current severity level of the patient's mental illness symptoms mandates that the patient's attendance at the group sessions will be necessary to prevent an inpatient psychiatric hospitalization.

Topic 3: Exploring Steps to Enhance Level of Self-Esteem

Exercise 4: Self-Nurturing

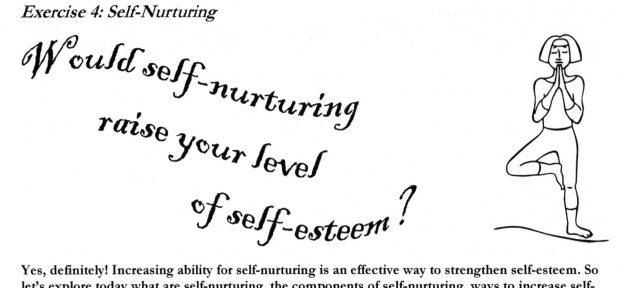

Would self-nurturing raise your level of self-esteem?

Yes, definitely! Increasing ability for self-nurturing is an effective way to strengthen self-esteem. So let's explore today what are self-nurturing, the components of self-nurturing, ways to increase self-nurturing, and potential benefits of self-nurturing.

- **Please answer at least two of the following questions:**[1]

    1. What is self-nurturing?
    2. What are the benefits of self-nurturing?
    3. What are the components of self-nurturing?
    4. What can be the important ingredients for good self-care?
    5. Can you identify at least three fun and relaxing things you like to do?
    6. How do you reward yourself?
    7. How do you celebrate your accomplishments?
    8. How can you forgive yourself?
    9. How can you use self-recognition?
    10. How should you nurture yourself even when you do not feel you deserve this?

---

[1] Answer key:
   1. Self-nurturing is a way of self-educating, promoting growth, and further developing oneself.
   2. Part of the answer is in the text above.
   3. They include six components: self-care, fun and relaxing things, self-reward, self-accomplishment, forgiving yourself, and self-recognition.
   4. Healthy eating and sleeping patterns, regular exercise, good hygiene, etc.
   5. They may include movie, massage, gardening, meditation, etc.
   6. Celebrating a good grade, spending time with a friend, and complimenting oneself for anything special that has been done.
   7. Keeping moments of accomplishments one is proud of, including a file of awards, certificates, etc.
   8. Do not be critical of oneself. We are not perfect!
   9. Treat oneself as though deserving to feel good and be nurtured.

Topic 3: Exploring Steps to Enhance Level of Self-Esteem

Exercise 5: Journaling

Purpose:

    A. To use journaling as a way to enhance self-esteem.

Hints and Procedures:

    While the handouts are being passed out, start the group session by reviewing journaling as an effective way to enhance self-esteem. Review the definition of self-nurturing. Encourage the members to use journaling with self-nurturing, and recognize personal strengths or accomplishments, which, as a result, can enhance their levels of self-esteem.

Group Session Model:

    This group session consisted of assisting and encouraging the members to use journaling as a way to enhance their self-esteem. The members were instructed to use handouts with a model containing past examples about self-nurturing and a personal strengths or accomplishments journal. Each member was challenged to identify at least one recent activity or behavior that was self-nurturing and at least one recent activity involving a personal strength or accomplishment. The clinician compared the feelings elicited by the group and summarized the result of the activities.

    The patient had marginal hygiene, fair eye contact, and fair participation in the group discussion. The patient was initially isolated from his peers with a sad facial expression and rigid posture, which suggested a continuous dominant depressive mental status. However, the patient was able to complete the group task, engage in the group discussion with moderate prompting, and share ideas on the subjected discussed. The patient shared with the members two past activities and his strengths involved with the comment, "Last Sunday, I had lunch with my best friend. Then I played the guitar and sang some of my favorite songs. I felt proud and relaxed."

    The patient received positive feedback related to his self-nurturing and accomplishment. The patient was receptive to his peers' feedback and responded positively to the clinician's intervention.

    The staff recommended that the patient will need to continue attending group sessions until he reaches his mood stabilization.

Topic 3: Exploring Steps to Enhance Level of Self-Esteem

Exercise 5: Journaling

There are many ways to increase levels of self-esteem. Journaling is an effective way to enhance your level of self-esteem. There are at least two ways to use journaling to raise your level of self-esteem: by self-nurturing and by recognizing personal strengths or accomplishments. The model below is about the two ways to use journaling. It can help you to develop the ability to use journaling in order to raise your level of self-esteem.

- Self-nurturing and recognition journaling model:

Self-nurturing	Strengths/accomplishments	Feelings
Aug 11, "I had lunch with my best friend.	Then I played the guitar and sang."	Proud, relaxed
Aug 12, "I jogged because I was stressed."	Self-caring	Relaxed

- By using the model above, try to identify at least one recent activity or behavior that was self-nurturing and at least one recent activity involving a personal strength.

    1. One of my recent activities or behaviors that was self-nurturing was _____
    2. One of my feelings elicited by this activity was _____
    3. One of my recent activities involving a personal strength was _____
    4. One of my feelings elicited by this activity was _____

- Now, continue to use journaling on a daily basis. Remember, by journaling, you can monitor how much you are progressing; you feel proud of yourself, and as a result, it can help you raise your level of self-esteem.

Topic 3: Exploring Steps to Enhance Level of Self-Esteem

Exercise 6: The Steps

Purpose:

    A. To identify appropriate steps to enhance levels of self-esteem.
    B. To explore ideas to raise levels of self-esteem.

Hints and Procedures:

Provide the members with the handouts and ask a member to read the caption about self-esteem. Promote a brief discussion by using the information from the caption. Encourage the members to explore ideas from the list as steps to enhance their levels of self-esteem. Discuss the benefits of each idea and how to put them into action.

Group Session Model:

The focus of this group session was to encourage the members to explore steps to enhance their levels of self-esteem. The clinician started the session by briefly reviewing the importance of maintaining a high level of self-esteem for good mental health, a positive attitude, and stabilization. Then the members were given handouts with a list of several ideas that can help raise levels of self-esteem. The group discussion focused on how to put the ideas into action.

During the session, the patient exhibited symptoms suggesting depression, such as flat affect, withdrawal, a dysphoric mood, and a sad facial expression. The patient required moderate prompting and encouragement to become involved in the group discussion. He commented on one activity from the list as follows: "I think I need to change my way of thinking and start practicing daily positive affirmations to help me think in a more positive way."

Positive feedback and encouragement were provided by the members regarding the patient's idea, to which he was receptive. Also, the patient agreed to explore other steps to enhance his level of self-esteem discussed by the members.

The staff will continue to assist the patient to implement effective steps to enhance his level of self-esteem and better control his mental illness symptoms.

26 ■ *Group Self-Esteem*

Topic 3: Exploring Steps to Enhance Level of Self-Esteem

Exercise 6: The Steps

"A high level of self-esteem is important for good mental health, a positive attitude, and stabilization. When the self-esteem is low, it is more difficult to deal with daily life stresses and life problems."

- **Complete the tasks below:**

    ◆ The ideas below are valuable steps to enhance your level of self-esteem. Select one that is attractive to you.

    ☐ 1. Developing personal goals
    ☐ 2. Working on hobbies
    ☐ 3. Developing arts
    ☐ 4. Focusing on positive thoughts
    ☐ 5. Greeting people pleasantly
    ☐ 6. Changing my lifestyle
    ☐ 7. Smiling more often
    ☐ 8. Making new friends
    ☐ 9. Working on a personal project
    ☐ 10. Participating in available activities
    ☐ 11. Paying special attention to grooming
    ☐ 12. Focusing on positive qualities
    ☐ 13. Changing my behaviors (specify)
    ☐ 14. Improving character
    ☐ 15. Practicing daily positive affirmations
    ☐ 16. Other _____

    ◆ Now, tell us at least one reason why this idea is attractive to you:
    Reason 1: _____
    Reason 2: _____

    ◆ Finally, how can you put this idea into action?

Topic 4: Using Self-Exploration to Increase Self-Esteem

Exercise 1: Positive Inner Messages

Purpose:

    A. To improve self-esteem by searching for positive inner messages.

Hints and Procedures:

    Distribute the handouts provided below. In order to search for positive inner messages, suggest to the members to use the phrase, "Looking inside myself now, I can find ..." Encourage the members to select and internalize positive messages from the list and comment on the meaning of each selection.

Group Session Model:

    The group session was developed with the purpose of training the members in the use of positive inner messages to improve their self-esteem. The members were asked to use handouts with a list of several positive messages. They were encouraged to select and internalize the positive messages by using the phrase, "Looking inside myself now, I can find ..." Also, the meaning of each positive message was commented on by the members.

    During the session, the patient appeared to be depressed. He was isolated from his peers, with a guarded behavior, sad facial expression, and rigid posture. The patient participated with minimal prompting. He completed the phrase as follows: "Looking inside myself now, I can find motivation in order to cope with my problems and finish this program."

    The clinician provided the patient with positive feedback and information designed to enable him to take steps to continue increasing his self-esteem. The patient was receptive to the feedback received and was open to suggestions.

    The staff has recommended that the patient will need treatment in order to continue improving his self-esteem and decreasing mental illness symptoms.

Topic 4: Using Self-Exploration to Increase Self-Esteem

Exercise 1: Positive Inner Messages

One effective way to get motivation for what we want to achieve in life is to search for positive inner messages. Positive inner messages are like energy that we need in order to move in the right direction. Searching for positive inner messages should be an important strategy in the process of increasing your level of self-esteem.

- **Try to complete the following:**

    Looking inside myself now, I can find ...

    1. peace of mind.
    2. changes that I have been making.
    3. determination to change.
    4. fun things.
    5. hope to get rid of my depression.
    6. motivation to cope with my problems.
    7. the possibility of living a better life.
    8. the potential to improve.
    9. the potential to keep sober.
    10. the power to overcome my problems.
    11. the release of negative feelings.
    12. an honest person.
    13. a nice person with a beautiful family.
    14. desire to get myself more active.
    15. faith in my higher power.
    16. God inside myself.
    17. the motivation to improve myself.
    18. the openness to change any of my bad behaviors.
    19. the potential to maintain stability.
    20. the potential to be okay.
    21. the potential to recover.
    22. the persistence to stabilize.
    23. the ability to cope with my mental illness.
    24. other _____

    ❖ What do such messages mean to you?

Topic 4: Using Self-Exploration to Increase Self-Esteem

Exercise 2: Positive "I Statements"

Purpose:

    A. To improve self-esteem by practicing positive "I statements."

Hints and Procedures:

    Provide the members with the handouts. Warm up the group discussion by asking the members for examples of positive "I statements." Encourage the members to pick up positive "I statements" from the list, or they can create their own. Promote the group discussion by using the content of each message including their meanings, benefits, and how they can make the messages become true.

Group Session Model:

    The group session aimed at training the members in the use of positive "I statements" as a way to improve their self-esteem. In order to facilitate the group activity, discussion, and process, the members were encouraged to use handouts with a list of several positive "I statements." They were encouraged to start using the statements on a daily basis.

    The patient came to the group session depressed. He was initially isolated from his peers, with guarded and suspicious behaviors, and tense posture. Upon being prompted by the clinician, the patient shared his own positive "I statement" by stating, "I am a nice person."

    The group intervention consisted of providing each other with positive reinforcement, to which the patient was receptive. Also, the patient agreed to continue practicing other positive "I statements" on a daily basis.

    The professional team will continue to help the patient practice the "I statements" technique daily to improve his self-esteem and functional level.

Topic 4: Using Self-Exploration to Increase Self-Esteem

Exercise 2: Positive "I Statements"

The use of positive "I statements" on a daily basis can be a very effective way to improve your level of self-esteem. It is a good idea to start the day with something powerful, and it is a good idea to develop daily healthy habits in life to stay positive. So, let's practice this technique today.

- **Please answer the following questions:**

    ◆ What can you say about yourself?

    1. I am competent.
    2. I am clean and sober.
    3. I am blessed to be here.
    4. I am blessed to have a place to live.
    5. I am a nice person.
    6. I have been succeeding in improving myself.
    7. I can see many good things.
    8. I can find some level of friendship.
    9. I want to love people and help them.
    10. I will stay in a good mood today.
    11. I am _____
    12. I have _____
    13. I can _____
    14. I want _____
    15. I will _____

    ◆ Why can you say that about yourself?

    ◆ How can you make this message become true?

Topic 4: Using Self-Exploration to Increase Self-Esteem

Exercise 3: Favorite Things

Purpose:

    A. To raise levels of self-esteem by sharing favorite things.

Hints and Procedures:

    Initiate the group discussion by reviewing the importance of sharing favorite things among people. Distribute the handouts provided below; encourage and assist the members to share their favorite things. Promote the group discussion about the positive feelings associated with the members' favorite things.

Group Session Model:

    The group session focused on encouraging and assisting the members to share favorite things. The clinician initiated the group discussion by reviewing with the members that sharing favorite things among people may be a good way to raise their levels of self-esteem. To facilitate the group discussion, the members were asked to use handouts with several questions related to favorite things. The group discussion focused on the positive feelings elicited by the favorite things.

    The patient had a low energy level, lack of motivation, and difficulty concentrating. The patient was responsive to the group activity only upon direct prompting from the clinician. The patient shared one of his favorite things by commenting, "This chain was a very special gift from my mother, and every time I use it, I feel proud of keeping it for so many years."

    Positive feedback and comments were provided by the members related to the patient's special necklace, for which he was very thankful.

    The professional team will continue to assist and motivate the patient to raise his level of self-esteem using self-disclosure.

Topic 4: Using Self-Exploration to Increase Self-Esteem

Exercise 3: Favorite Things

My Favorite Pet and my Special Possessions

Sharing favorite things among people can make you feel proud of them, and as a result, it can help you raise your level of self-esteem. Today, you will have the opportunity to start sharing with your peers some of your favorite things. We want to know more about you.

- Please answer at least two of the following questions:

    1. What is your favorite pet or animal? Why?
    2. What is your special possession? Why?
    3. What is your favorite clothing? Why?
    4. What are your favorite shoes? Why?
    5. What is your favorite holiday? Why?
    6. What is your favorite place? Why?
    7. What is your favorite vacation? Why?
    8. What is your favorite food? Why?
    9. What is your favorite drink? Why?
    10. What is your favorite moment in life? Why?

Topic 4: Using Self-Exploration to Increase Self-Esteem

Exercise 4: Personal Hobbies

Purpose:

    A. To improve self-esteem by exploring personal hobbies.

Hints and Procedures:

    Warm up the group discussion by reviewing some benefits of developing personal hobbies. Distribute the handouts provided below, and continue the group discussion by assisting and encouraging the members to explore their personal hobbies. Summarize the benefits of the session.

Group Session Model:

    The group session focused on helping and encouraging the members to explore personal hobbies to improve their self-esteem. The members were provided with handouts with a word find exercise and questions related to several activities suggesting hobbies. They were asked to identify past and present activities they would like to be involved in as hobbies.

    The patient came to the session appropriately dressed, clean, well groomed, and with fair eye contact, and was responsive to prompting. The patient stated, "I do not have any hobby at the present due to my severe depression, but I would like to start painting again."

    The patient's plan was reinforced by the members. He was receptive to the reinforcement. Also, the patient was receptive to the group discussion about becoming involved in several other hobbies in the community.

    The staff has determined that the patient will need this level of service in order to continue improving his level of self-esteem and reaching mood stabilization.

Topic 4: Using Self-Exploration to Increase Self-Esteem

Exercise 4: Personal Hobbies

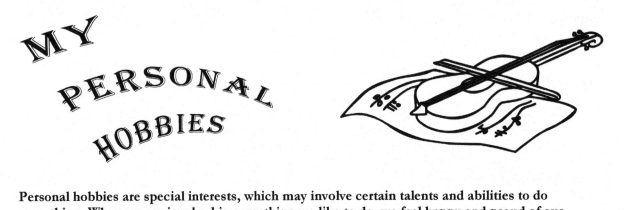

Personal hobbies are special interests, which may involve certain talents and abilities to do something. When we are involved in something we like to do, we feel happy and proud of our accomplishments. As a result, it helps us enhance our levels of self-esteem.

- Can you answer at least one of the questions below?

    1. Do you possess any special talent? What is it?
    2. Do you have any special interest? What is it?
    3. What are your personal hobbies?
    4. What hobbies have you done in the past?
    5. Can you identify one of your hobbies in the word find puzzle below?[1]
    6. Are you currently involved in this hobby? If not, why?
    7. What do you need to do to get involved in this hobby?
    8. How does this hobby help you improve your level of self-esteem?
    9. Can you identify at least one positive feeling related to this hobby?
    10. Where in the community can you get involved in this hobby?

N	E	E	D	L	E	P	O	I	N	T	Y	M	E	C	H	A	N	I	C
P	A	I	N	T	I	N	G	L	A	N	G	U	A	G	E	S	C	H	H
A	G	A	R	D	E	N	I	N	G	F	I	S	H	I	N	G	A	R	U
I	D	R	A	W	I	N	G	R	E	A	D	I	N	G	D	A	N	C	R
N	R	E	S	T	O	R	A	T	I	O	N	C	E	R	A	M	I	C	C
D	A	N	C	I	N	G	F	I	S	H	A	N	T	I	Q	U	E	S	H

---

[1] Keywords: antiques, ceramic, church, dancing, drawing, fishing, gardening, languages, mechanic, music, needlepoint, painting, reading, restoration.

Topic 5: Exploring Positive Attributes

Exercise 1: Positive Attributes

Purpose:

    A. To identify positive attributes to improve self-esteem.
    B. To practice daily affirmations of positive attributes.

Hints and Procedures:

While the handouts are being passed out, ask a group member to volunteer to read the text related to personal positive attributes. Encourage and assist the members to answer the questions related to positive attributes as well as to practice them on a daily basis. Provide the members with positive reinforcement for their positive attributes and related feelings.

Group Session Model:

The clinician initiated the group discussion about how positive attributes can help improve self-esteem and how people often have difficulty expressing their positive attributes. Handouts with information and questions related to positive attributes were provided. The members were challenged to develop a list of their positive attributes and were encouraged to start practicing them on a daily basis.

The patient's dominant mood appeared depressed and withdrawn, as he isolated himself from the group, had poor eye contact, and had non-spontaneous speech. The clinician assisted the patient with clarification and instructions in order to identify his positive attributes. The patient shared with the members one of his positive attributes by stating, "I think one of my strengths is that I am a creative person."

The patient received positive reinforcement and support from the members regarding his positive attribute. The patient responded positively to the reinforcement and seemed receptive to the group discussion about other important information related to the topic discussed.

The patient has not yet reached the baseline of improvement, and continued attendance to this level of service is necessary to help him prevent deterioration of his mental illness symptoms or psychiatric inpatient hospitalization.

Topic 5: Exploring Positive Attributes

Exercise 1: Positive Attributes

My Positive Attributes

Identifying positive attributes is an effective way to improve levels of self-esteem. Some people find this difficult to do, but with the use of daily positive affirmations and persistence, it can be done. Today, you will be challenged to develop a list of your positive attributes. Be patient! This may take time!

- Can you answer at least two of the questions below?

    1. What are your strengths?
    2. What are your assets?
    3. What are your abilities?
    4. What success have you had in your life?
    5. What are the things you are good at?
    6. What are the things you are grateful for?
    7. What are the things that are going well for you?
    8. What are the things you have overcome?
    9. What are the things you have cared about?
    10. What are the things you like about yourself?

    ✧ How do you feel talking about these two positive attributes?

Topic 5: Exploring Positive Attributes

Exercise 2: Positive Traits

Purpose:

    A. To increase self-esteem by focusing on positive traits.

Hints and Procedures:

Distribute the handouts provided below. Encourage and assist the members to use the words from the list to describe their positive traits. Promote positive comments following the identification of each trait: Why do members give the positive traits to themselves? How can the positive traits help them succeed in life?

Group Session Model:

The clinician initiated the group discussion by emphasizing the importance of focusing on positive traits as a valuable way to increase levels of self-esteem. In order to facilitate the group activity, the members were given handouts with a list of several positive words. Each member was asked to identify at least one word and provide a comment about how that word would describe his or her positive traits.

The patient had a dominant depressive mental status. He sat back quietly and mostly like an observer. However, when directly approached, his participation was appropriate. The clinician prompted the patient to identify his positive traits. The patient commented on one trait by stating, "I am a loving person, and this positive trait makes me feel proud of myself."

The members empathized with the patient's feeling and reinforced his positive trait. The patient was receptive to the support received. Also, the patient had an opportunity to learn about various words supporting positive traits and agreed to explore them in the future to describe other personal positive traits.

The plan for the future sessions is to continue to provide the patient with further therapeutic approaches until the patient reaches mood stabilization.

Topic 5: Exploring Positive Attributes

Exercise 2: Positive Traits

What are your positive traits?

Positive traits are important ingredients to enhance levels of self-esteem, and there are many words that can describe positive traits. Below is a list of them.

- Please choose at least one word from the list below that can describe one of your positive traits and complete the statements as follows:

  ⬥ I am ...

1. courteous.	16. artistic.	31. appreciative.	46. accurate.
2. analytical.	17. adaptable.	32. caring.	47. cooperative.
3. affectionate.	18. creative.	33. considerate.	48. polite.
4. consistent.	19. capable.	34. competent.	49. confident.
5. disciplined.	20. diligent.	35. determined.	50. dynamic.
6. efficient.	21. enthusiastic.	36. energetic.	51. easygoing.
7. empathic.	22. fair.	37. flexible.	52. forgiving.
8. friendly.	23. funny.	38. paternal.	53. maternal.
9. generous.	24. gentle.	39. glad.	54. honest.
10. hospitable.	25. helpful.	40. humorous.	55. idealistic.
11. industrious.	26. intelligent.	41. imaginative.	56. kind.
12. loveable.	27. likable.	42. mature.	57. neat.
13. natural.	28. nurturing.	43. persevering.	58. persistent.
14. compassionate.	29. realistic.	44. reliable.	59. rational.
15. sincere.	30. sensitive.	45. tolerant.	60. unique.

  ⬥ This positive trait can help me to succeed in life because
  _____

Topic 5: Exploring Positive Attributes

Exercise 3: Special Talents

Purpose:

    A. To nurture positive self-esteem by discovering special talents.
    B. To discuss concepts related to talents.

Hints and Procedures:

While the handouts are being distributed, introduce the idea of nurturing positive self-esteem with talents. Ask the members to think about their talents. They may include anything special done in the past or present.

Group Session Model:

The group session was on special talents. Handouts with questions about talents were passed out. During the first part of the group discussion, the members were encouraged to discuss concepts related to talents. During the second part of the group activity, the members were asked to share their talents including anything special done in the past or present. The focus of the group discussion was about nurturing positive self-esteem by discovering special talents.

In prior sessions, the patient came to the group depressed. Similarly, in this session, the patient was observed to have downcast eyes, be isolated, and have a sad and tearful facial expression. However, the patient was able to follow instructions and made appropriate comments related to the topic discussed. He stated, "I believe that talent is unique for each person, because we are all different." Also, the patient shared with his peers one of his previous talents by stating, "I used to sew before. I used to do very beautiful clothes, and that was one of my best talents."

Positive social reinforcement was provided by the members in response to the patient's previous talent. The patient responded positively to the reinforcement as well as demonstrated an understanding about the concepts related to talents discussed during the group discussion.

The future sessions will focus on assisting and encouraging the patient to continue exploring activities of personal interest, such as talents, as part of his stabilization process.

Topic 5: Exploring Positive Attributes

Exercise 3: Special Talents

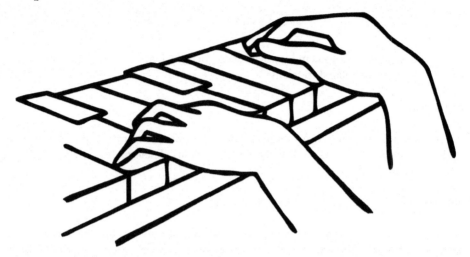

You can nurture positive self-esteem by discovering what you are good at doing. Part of your self-esteem comes from feeling competent and skilled at something you enjoy.

- **Let's discuss some concepts of talents with the questions below:**[1]

    1. What is a talent?
    2. What do talents have to do with skill?
    3. Where does talent come from?
    4. Does everybody have talent? Explain.
    5. How can talents be discovered?
    6. Can talents be changed? Why?
    7. What is the relationship between talents and gifts?
    8. What is one of your best talents?
    9. What special thing have you done in the past?
    10. How do you feel from possessing this talent?

---

[1] Answer key:
1. A talent is a special ability or gift, a special creative or artistic aptitude.
2. They have nothing to do with skills.
3. Talents are born with people.
4. Yes, everybody is unique and has something special.
5. By personally trying, being exposed, and being observed by others.
6. Talents are not changeable.
7. Talents are like gifts because we receive them.

Topic 5: Exploring Positive Attributes

Exercise 4: Self-Worth

Purpose:

    A. To recognize self-worth in order to improve self-esteem.
    B. To provide positive reinforcement for self-worth among group members.

Hints and Procedures:

Provide the members with the handouts below. Read the text and warm up the group discussion with its information. Continue the group discussion by using the attached questions. Provide the members with positive reinforcement for their positive statements related to self-worth.

Group Session Model:

The group session focused on providing the members with positive reinforcement for their self-worth in order to improve their self-esteem. The clinician initiated the group session by reviewing some concepts related to self-worth. The members were given handouts with questions related to self-worth and the group discussion focused on the content of the questions.

The patient spoke in a hesitant manner, was constantly fidgeting, had an anxious mood, and had sad facial expression. The patient was able to contribute to the group discussion by answering one of the questions for himself. The patient stated, "Despite being mentally ill, I get along well with everybody."

The clinician assisted the patient in reflecting on the benefits of the session. During the group discussion, the members discussed how increased insight into personal values allows greater potential for self-worth and increased self-esteem. The patient remained attentive to the group discussion.

The future sessions will continue to provide the patient with the opportunity to explore other personal values and strengths as part of the process to improve his level of self-esteem.

Topic 5: Exploring Positive Attributes

Exercise 4: Self-Worth

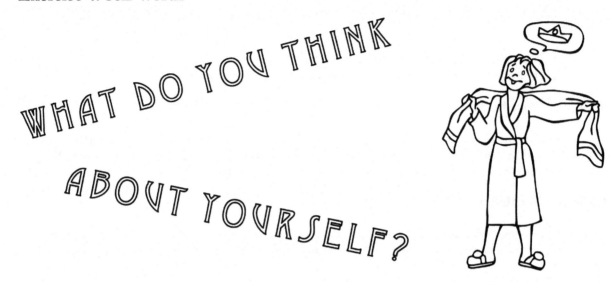

Your opinion and attitudes toward your personal values as a person, strengths, weaknesses, and purposes in life may lead to a high or low self-worth. A high level of self-worth is associated with confidence, happiness, motivation, and security. It can lead to success, greater productivity, and a high level of self-esteem. So, it is very important to know more about yourself.

- Let's try to answer the questions below:

    1. What is self-worth?[1]
    2. Is your self-worth high or low? Why?
    3. What do you think about yourself?
    4. What is your value as a person?
    5. What do you plan to achieve in your life?
    6. What is your place in this world?
    7. How do you get along with others?
    8. Are you an independent or dependent person? Why?
    9. Can you describe at least two of your strengths?
    10. Can you describe one of your weaknesses?

---

[1] Self-worth is the unconditional value we place on ourselves. It is how we appear to ourselves. It is based on what others think of us and what we think of others. Self-worth is an overall measure of how much we value ourselves and give priority to our own needs and happiness.

Topic 5: Exploring Positive Attributes

Exercise 5: Personal Strengths

Purpose:

    A. To recognize strengths in a creative and structured format.
    B. To identify strengths in five life dimensions.

Hints and Procedures:

Distribute the handouts provided below. Warm up the group discussion with the information provided. Assist and encourage the members to explore their strengths in the five life dimensions by answering the attached questions.

Group Session Model:

The clinician warmed up the group discussion by reviewing some benefits related to personal strengths. Then handouts containing information related to personal strengths were distributed, and the members were asked to answer questions in order to identify their strengths. The clinician focused intervention on assisting and encouraging the members to identify strengths in the following five life dimensions: physical, social, spiritual, intellectual, and professional.

The patient was somewhat guarded, isolated, and sad. However, he presented himself in a kempt and clean manner. Upon being prompted and on approach, the patient chose the spiritual dimension strength to talk about and commented, "I am a spiritually oriented person. I believe that God will give me the strength and courage to overcome any obstacle related to my mental condition. So, I can succeed in life."

The clinician reflected on the patient's thoughts, provided feedback, and educated the patient on how recognizing personal strengths can raise his level of self-esteem. The patient was receptive to the therapeutic intervention.

The professional team has recommended that the patient will need to continue to be assisted with further therapeutic interventions to explore his personal strengths in other life dimensions.

Topic 5: Exploring Positive Attributes

Exercise 5: Personal Strengths

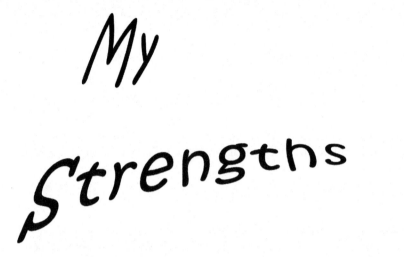

We can do well in many different life dimensions, but we need strengths to do well or to succeed in any area. Strengths provide us with energy to move on. They help us overcome negative feelings including disappointments, frustrations, and low self-worth. They help us raise our levels of self-esteem. What is your opinion?

- Below, you are going to have an opportunity to explore your own strengths in the following five different life dimensions: physical, social, spiritual, intellectual, and professional. Try to be honest with yourself and answer all the questions the best you can.

    1. What are your physical strengths?
    2. Which one is the most important to you? Why?
    3. How is your social life?
    4. Do you have any special social skill? (Describe it!)
    5. What is your spiritual orientation?
    6. Do you have any special spiritual ability? (Describe it!)
    7. Do you have any special intellectual ability?
    8. What is an intellectual activity you like to do?
    9. Do you have any professional skills? How is that?
    10. How can we develop personal strengths?

Topic 5: Exploring Positive Attributes

Exercise 6: Positive Qualities

Purpose:

    A. To identify positive qualities among group members.
    B. To accept positive qualities as a way to increase self-esteem.

Hints and Procedures:

Explain to the members that identifying and accepting positive qualities can be a very powerful way to improve their self-esteem. The patients can be surprised to learn about their positive qualities through comments by other members. The activity can be an enjoyable and powerful way of making the members feeling good about themselves.

Group Session Model:

This group session's objective was to identify positive qualities among the members. The activity consisted of having the members completing phrases describing positive qualities of each other. To facilitate the group activity, the clinician prepared small pieces of papers with several different uncompleted phrases related to positive qualities, with the names of each member, and distributed the papers randomly to the members. The members were asked to complete the phrases. The member with his or her name on the paper was asked to make a brief comment whether he or she accepts or agrees with that phrase.

The patient's mood and affect was depressed with symptoms similar to the previous sessions, including lack of motivation, withdrawal, sadness, and isolation. The patient was able to participate with moderate prompting and was able to complete the group task. A member of the group commented on the patient's good listening quality, and the patient replied, "This is true. I am a good listener, and this has been helping me to learn more about myself by listening attentively to other people while they are talking to me."

Positive social reinforcement was provided by the members in the form of applause in response to the patient's positive quality, to which he was receptive.

The staff will continue to work on raising the patient's level of self-esteem by focusing on his positive qualities.

Topic 5: Exploring Positive Attributes

Exercise 6: Positive Qualities

- **Instructions to the Group Leader**

Before starting the group self-esteem session, photocopy this page and write the name of each group member in the spaces below. Cut out the squares and put them inside a hat or cup. Randomly, ask the members to pick up the small pieces of paper and complete the statements. Make sure that nobody picks up his or her own name. Then encourage the members to read the phrases one by one. After each reading, ask the person named on the small paper to make a brief comment about his or her positive quality written by the other member (e.g., if he or she accepts or agrees with that quality or does not, as well as his or her feelings related to that quality).

Name:	Name:	Name:	Name:
I know that you will succeed in …	I respect you because you always …	I like to be your friend because …	I like to hear when you …

Name:	Name:	Name:	Name:
I admire you for …	I like the way you …	I like you because …	You are a good …

Name:	Name:	Name:	Name:
You look good when …	You have a natural talent for …	You know how to …	You have a great …

Name:	Name:	Name:	Name:
You have the potential for …	You make me feel good because …	You can make …	You have a pretty …

Name:	Name:	Name:	Name:
You are always …	You can provide us with …	One of your positive traits is …	One thing you do well is …

Topic 5: Exploring Positive Attributes

Exercise 7: Potential to Excel

Purpose:

    A. To give and receive positive statements about the potential to excel.
    B. To explore areas to excel.

Hints and Procedures:

Areas where a person can excel may include the social, spiritual, intellectual, mental, physical, physiological, and professional. During the group discussion, ask the members about how they would help each other excel in these areas (e.g., by giving suggestions, advice, encouragement, and positive feedback).

Group Session Model:

The group session aimed at encouraging the members to give and receive positive statements to each other. To facilitate the group activity, the clinician randomly distributed small pieces of paper with the names of each member containing the following incomplete statement: "You have the potential to excel in ..." Then the members were asked to complete the statements. After completing and reading each statement, positive social reinforcement was provided by the members to each other in the form of applause for how each member could excel.

The patient manifested signs suggesting a depressive mental status. Among them, the patient was observed as guarded, with a rigid posture, and a sad and tearful facial expression. After some prompting, the patient stated, "Yes, I feel that I have the potential to excel in my social life, because I am a social person."

The patient was receptive to the members' reinforcement and other comments. Also, the patient showed interest in succeeding in other different areas being explored by the members, including the following: intellectual, mental, physical, physiological, professional, and spiritual.

The staff will continue to encourage the patient to explore other areas in which to excel in order to elevate his level of self-esteem.

Topic 5: Exploring Positive Attributes

Exercise 7: Potential to Excel

- **Instructions to the Group Leader**

    Photocopy this page and write the name of each group member on the top of the small squares. Cut out the squares, fold them, and put them into a cup or container. Each member is chosen to draw one name from the cup or container and complete the statement. Make sure that nobody picks up his or her own name. Then the members start announcing the persons' names one by one and reading the statements. After each reading, ask the members to come up with other ideas about other areas in which they think that person can excel. Provide each member with applause and other positive feedback for the areas in which each person can excel.

You have the potential to excel in:	You have the potential to excel in:	You have the potential to excel in:	You have the potential to excel in:
You have the potential to excel in:	You have the potential to excel in:	You have the potential to excel in:	You have the potential to excel in:
You have the potential to excel in:	You have the potential to excel in:	You have the potential to excel in:	You have the potential to excel in:
You have the potential to excel in:	You have the potential to excel in:	You have the potential to excel in:	You have the potential to excel in:
You have the potential to excel in:	You have the potential to excel in:	You have the potential to excel in:	You have the potential to excel in:

Topic 6: Exploring Self-Accomplishments

Exercise 1: Past Self-Accomplishments

Purpose:

    A. To increase self-esteem by identifying past self-accomplishments.
    B. To provide group feedback and meanings for past self-achievements.

Hints and Procedures

Use the handouts provided below to facilitate the members' identification of past accomplishments. What types of work have they done? Ask for details about their accomplishments. They may include raising a family, creating a new recipe, making jewelry, learning a dance step, learning to make a dress, helping a friend, etc. List the accomplishments on the blackboard. Comment on the collective expertise presented in the group.

Group Session Model:

The purpose of this group session was to encourage the members to identify and focus on their past accomplishments as a way to increase their levels of self-esteem. To facilitate the group discussion, the members were asked to use handouts with questions and a list of several activities related to self-accomplishments. The treatment intervention consisted of providing each member with positive reinforcement for their accomplishments and comments on the collective expertise presented in the group.

The patient displayed a flat facial expression, a low-key demeanor, limited insight, and difficulty with concentration. The patient shared with the members one of his accomplishments as follows: "Well, one of my accomplishments was in school when I used to work as a volunteer helping other kids."

The members supported and gave credit for the patient's past accomplishment. Although events in his life seemed to have reduced his self-importance, the patient recognized that he has made some accomplishments in the past that have increased his level of self-esteem.

The future sessions will continue to provide the patient with positive feedback and meanings for other accomplishments.

Topic 6: Exploring Self-Accomplishments

Exercise 1: Past Self-Accomplishments

The Greatest Accomplishments in my Life

Taking credit for our successes and accomplishments in the past can be an effective way to help us increase our levels of self-esteem.

- What have been your prior accomplishments?

- Please answer at least three questions below.

    ✧ Can you identify one thing that you do better than anyone else?
    ✧ Which special dishes have you been able to cook?
    ✧ Which special work have you done?
    ✧ Have you ever ...

1. made soap?	13. attended a bull fight?	25. caught lightning bugs?
2. played football?	14. climbed a tree?	26. created a new dish?
3. played soccer?	15. chopped down a tree?	27. gone bobsledding?
4. saved a sick pet?	16. gone tobogganing?	28. gone Christmas caroling?
5. jumped into a pile of leaves?	17. talked on the radio?	29. kept a diary?
6. made a campfire?	18. made a toy?	30. added others you think of?
7. made sun tea?	19. flew an airplane?	31. danced the Charleston?
8. played horseshoes?	20. played on a softball team?	32. danced the cha-cha?
9. pressed leaves?	21. rode a scooter?	33. danced the tango?
10. served on a jury?	22. talked on TV?	34. danced the samba?
11. used a telescope?	23. visited a national park?	35. worked on ceramics?
12. written a poem?	24. written a song?	36. written a story?

- Now, tell us: how was your experience? What have you learned from that?

Topic 6: Exploring Self-Accomplishments

Exercise 2: Ongoing Self-Accomplishments

Purpose:

    A. To identify ongoing self-accomplishments.

Hints and Procedures:

While the handouts are being passed out, promote the initial group discussion with the concepts "focusing on the here and now" and "from now on ..." Encourage the members to complete the statements related to their ongoing accomplishments. Review the benefits of the activity and the use of self-accomplishments to enhance levels of self-esteem.

Group Session Model:

The clinician initiated the group session by introducing the idea of identifying ongoing self-accomplishments to increase levels of self-esteem. The members were provided with handouts containing information and incomplete statements to facilitate the identification of their ongoing accomplishments. The members were asked to complete the following statements: "In the here and now, I am working on ..."; "From now on, I will work on ..."; and "I will continue doing that by ..."

The patient appeared sad, distracted, and isolated. Also, his depressed mood had been apparent in prior sessions. He required prompting and encouragement to participate in the group activity and discussion. In response to the group task, the patient stated, "In the here and now, I am working on my recovery, and from now on, I will focus on things that I need to do to develop my own independence. I will continue doing that by being persistent."

The patient was provided with positive feedback, reassurance, and reinforcement for his statements, to which he responded positively.

The staff will focus on helping and encouraging the patient to continue working on his ongoing accomplishments in order to build up a high level of self-esteem.

Topic 6: Exploring Self-Accomplishments

Exercise 2: Ongoing Self-Accomplishments

The process of self-accomplishment should be a continuous activity in your life. It is a good way of enhancing your level of self-esteem. "Focusing on the here and now" and "from now on" can help you with this process. Ongoing self-accomplishments may include completing previous projects, making upcoming holiday preparations, and planning special upcoming events.

- Please, complete the following statements:

    ✧ In the here and now, I am working on

    _____

    ✧ From now on, I will work on

    _____

    ✧ I will continue doing that by

    _____

Topic 7: Improving Self-Image

Exercise 1: Self-Image Components

Purpose:

    A. To explore components of self-image.
    B. To discuss concepts related to self-image.

Hints and Procedures:

Distribute the handouts provided below. Use questions 1–3 to kick off the discussion with the corresponding answers. Continue the group discussion by exploring the five components of self-image. Use the content of each question related to self-image components to promote the group discussion.

Group Session Model:

This group session was aimed at helping the members to explore components of self-image. The clinician started the group discussion by reviewing some concepts related to self-image. Then the members were encouraged to answer questions about the following five components of self-image: physical, psychological, mental, social, and perceptional. The group discussion focused on the content of each question related to the self-image components.

The patient sat distant from the clinician and was tense in his body language. He showed low motivation, a sad facial expression, and limited interaction. The clinician assisted the patient to explore components of his self-image. The patient focused on his social component and expressed himself by saying, "Despite being currently isolated from everybody, I have many friends who care about me. I used to be a very social person."

The members encouraged the patient to return to his prior social behavior. The patient was receptive to the encouragement and recognized the importance of working on all five components of his self-image to enhance his level of self-esteem.

The future therapeutic interventions will continue to assist and encourage the patient in developing a consistent positive self-image and enhancing his level of self-esteem.

Topic 7: Improving Self-Image

Exercise 1: Self-Image Components

Improving a personal self-image is a very important strategy to enhance a person's level of self-esteem. Self-image has at least five components to work on such as, physical, psychological, mental, social, and perceptional. It is very important to explore your self-image through these five components. Let's try to do that now.

- **Please answer the following questions:**

    1. What is self-image?[1]
    2. Which factors can affect self-image?[2]
    3. What is the connection between self-image and self-esteem?[3]
    4. What do you think you look like physically?
    5. What do you know about your psychological state—for instance, your personality?
    6. What does being "mentally stable" mean for you?
    7. What kind of person do you think you are: social or introverted?
    8. What do you think others think of you? Why?
    9. How much do you think others like you? Why?
    10. How do you get along with others?

---

[1] Self-image is how you see yourself in relation to others. This has a lot to do with your perception of yourself and how you see yourself physically, psychologically, mentally, and socially.

[2] It may be affected by many factors such as past experiences, failures, triumphs, humiliations, and breakthroughs.

[3] They are close to each other. Self-esteem focuses on how you feel about yourself. Self-image is about how you see yourself.

Topic 7: Improving Self-Image

Exercise 2: Self-Image Improvement

Purpose:

    A. To build up positive self-image.

Hints and Procedures:

    Start the group discussion with the following questions: Why is self-image important? How can we improve our self-images? Then ask the members to use the handouts provided below, and answer the questions to help them build up their positive self-images. Promote the group discussion with the content of each question related to self-image improvement.

Group Session Model:

    This group session focused on helping the members explore combined strategies to build up their positive self-images. The clinician initiated the group discussion by asking the members two questions: Why is self-image important? How can we improve our self-images? Then the members were asked to use handouts containing questions related to self-image improvement to facilitate the process of building up their positive self-images. The clinician guided the group activity by prompting each member to participate in the group discussion.

    During the group session, the patient was observed with increased attention and motivation for the group activity. The patient's affect appeared less depressed, and the patient was more involved in the group dynamic than before. He was observed interacting with peers with a more relaxed posture. The patient commented on one of the questions by stating, "I see myself as a polite and friendly person. The thing I like most about myself is my frankness."

    Positive reinforcement was provided by the members in the form of applause in response to the patient's positive qualities. The patient was receptive to the applause, and as a result, he agreed to work in the future on other strategies in order to continue improving his self-image.

    The professional team will continue to work on helping the patient to improve his self-image and self-esteem as part of his stabilization process.

Topic 7: Improving Self-Image

Exercise 2: Self-Image Improvement

Your self-image may be the product of your past experiences, failures, progress, humiliations, or accomplishments. How you can improve your self-image would depend on a combination of combined strategies involving changes. However, you also need to be persistent, consistent, and committed to do what you need to do. Are you ready to start?

- The questions below will help you discover the path for a positive self-image that you can build up for yourself.

    1. Can you identify at least three things you like about yourself?
    2. Can you make a list to include at least three good things people have said about you?
    3. Can you identify one of your negative thoughts?
    4. Can you identify at least one strategy to replace your negative thoughts?
    5. Can you think about at least one change you need to make? How can you do that?
    6. How can you become active?
    7. How can you increase your energy level?
    8. How can you feel better about yourself?
    9. How can you accept yourself the way you are?
    10. How can you recognize your weaknesses and work on overcoming them?
    11. What would be a big but realistic challenge for you?
    12. What are at least two goals for your future? How can you meet them?

Topic 7: Improving Self-Image

Exercise 3: The Five Senses

Purpose:

    A. To use the five senses to improve self-image.

Hints and Procedures:

Introduce the topic by asking the members to identify the five senses: vision, auditory, smell, taste, and touch. Encourage the members to use the handouts provided below to discuss how they can use their five senses to improve their self-images. Promote the group discussion with the content of each statement related to the five senses.

Group Session Model:

The objective of this group session was to encourage the members to use the five senses to improve their self-images. The clinician introduced the topic by stating the importance of having a positive self-image and how our senses can influence our self-images in a positive or negative way. The members were asked to use handouts and complete five statements related to the five senses in order to improve their self-images. The group discussion focused on the content of each statement.

The patient came to the group session neat and clean, but with a moderate level of depression as evidenced by his sad facial expression and initial isolated behavior. However, the patient interacted appropriately with his peers. With minimum prompting, the patient answered one of the questions by stating, "Well, with my ears, I can listen to people, learn, and take advice from them about how to improve my self-image."

The patient's idea was supported and encouraged by other members. The patient was receptive to the feedback. Also, he was in accordance with other members' suggestions on how to use their other senses to improve his self-image.

Based on the patient's current moderate depressive mental status, it is recommended that he continue to attend this level of service in order to improve his mental status and reach mood stabilization.

Topic 7: Improving Self-Image

Exercise 3: The Five Senses

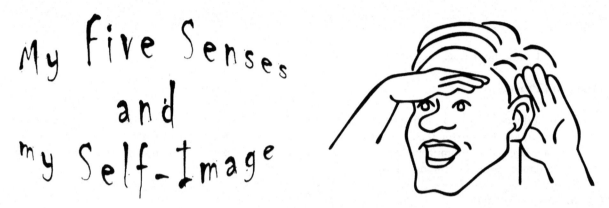

People get all their knowledge from their senses. Each sense collects information about the world and detects changes within the body. They can influence our self-images in a positive or negative way.

- How can you use your five senses to improve your self-image?

    ◆ With my eyes, I can _____

    ◆ With my ears, I can _____

    ◆ With my taste, I can _____

    ◆ By touching, I can _____

    ◆ By smiling, I can _____

Topic 7: Improving Self-Image

Exercise 4: Family Messages

Purpose:

A. To explore past family messages impacting self-image.

Hints and Procedures:

Provide the members with the handouts to facilitate the group discussion. The use of self-revelation of family messages, such as traditional sayings, can open the group members to feedback, which may help form a more positive self-image. Promote a group discussion about the positive and negative impact of the family messages on self-image. Determine which sayings are helpful and which ones should be replaced with more positive self-statements in forming a more positive self-image.

Group Session Model:

The purpose of this group session was to help the members to explore the impact of past family messages in the formation of self-image. The clinician introduced the topic of self-image and its relation to self-esteem. The members were provided with handouts with a list of popular sayings and were asked to discuss which ones are helpful and which ones should be replaced with more positive self-statements in the formation of a positive self-image.

The patient's mood was depressed and congruent with his affect. He was guarded and withdrawn, with limited interaction and limited participation. The patient chose the old saying "family problems should not be taken outside the home" and made the following comment: "This is an old saying, which is no longer true, because now we have psychologists and psychotherapists who can help us solve many problems inside the family."

The patient's opinion was supported by his peers. The patient responded positively to the feedback. The patient benefited from this group session by increasing awareness of how past family messages may be a set of negative or positive impacts on his current self-image.

The future therapeutic intervention will continue to assist the patient in developing a consistently positive self-image, which can lead to an increase in his level of self-esteem.

Topic 7: Improving Self-Image

Exercise 4: Family Messages

Your current self-image is connected to your early family messages including popular sayings and values. The negative or positive messages may have had an impact on your self-image. It is important to discuss with your peers what sayings are helpful and which ones should be replaced with more positive and realistic self-statements.

- Below, you will find a list of positive (P) and negative (N) messages from those old times. Identify the ones you know and discuss with your peers which sayings are positive and which ones you need to replace.

Popular saying: P   or   N?

1. "Family problems should not be taken outside the home."   ☐   ☐
2. "Children are to be seen and not to be heard."   ☐   ☐
3. "The grass is greener on the other side."   ☐   ☐
4. "Clumsy as a bull in a china closet."   ☐   ☐
5. "Into a closed mouth, flies do not enter."   ☐   ☐
6. "The early bird catches the worm."   ☐   ☐
7. "Old people should stay home."   ☐   ☐
8. "We are the fruit of our past."   ☐   ☐
9. "Think before speaking."   ☐   ☐
10. Your own saying: _____   ☐   ☐

✧ Why are the sayings above positive or negative?

Topic 7: Improving Self-Image

Exercise 5: Hygiene and Grooming

Purpose:

A. To increase self-image by improving personal hygiene and grooming.

Hints and Procedures:

Introduce the topic by reviewing with the members possible negative consequences related to poor personal hygiene and inappropriate grooming (e.g., bad body odor, bad breath, colds, gastroenteritis, infections, and poor self-image). Use the handouts provided below, and ask the members to determine the frequency of each activity related to personal hygiene and grooming. Promote the group discussion with the content of each activity.

Group Session Model:

The subject of this group session was on improving hygiene and grooming. At the beginning of the group session, the members were asked to identify areas of personal hygiene and grooming. They were asked to discuss possible negative consequences related to poor personal hygiene and inappropriate grooming. During the second part of the session, the members were encouraged to use handouts with a list of several activities for personal hygiene and grooming. The group discussion focused on the frequency of each activity, emphasizing the importance of maintaining personal hygiene and proper grooming habits to increase self-image.

Affects of depression were displayed by the patient during the session, which included sadness and initial isolation. Also, the patient was observed with a puzzled facial expression and sat hunched over. The patient stated, "Despite being depressed, I always take a daily shower and take good care of my body."

The patient received support from his peers regarding his daily shower. The patient was receptive to the feedback received and was able to share with the group other valuable ideas related to hygiene and grooming.

Based on the patient's current depressive mental status, he continues to need to attend this level of service to prevent any exacerbation of his mental illness symptoms, which may require psychiatric hospitalization.

Topic 7: Improving Self-Image

Exercise 5: Hygiene and Grooming

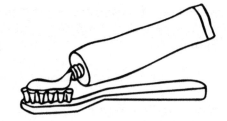

Personal hygiene is one of the first steps to good grooming and good health. It is an effective way we have to protect ourselves and others from illness. Maintaining your personal hygiene can enhance your physical and emotional well-being and increase your self-image.

- Today, you will have an opportunity to discuss personal hygiene and grooming routines. This will be a fun activity. So let's find out how much you know about this subject.

    ◆ I should ...

	2xWk	1xWk	Daily	2xDay	Other
1. brush my teeth	☐	☐	☐	☐	____
2. brush my shoes	☐	☐	☐	☐	____
3. change my socks	☐	☐	☐	☐	____
4. change my clothes	☐	☐	☐	☐	____
5. change pads, tampons, or menstrual devices	☐	☐	☐	☐	____
6. clean my room/apartment/house	☐	☐	☐	☐	____
7. comb my hair	☐	☐	☐	☐	____
8. cut my nails	☐	☐	☐	☐	____
9. insert odor-eater insoles in my shoes	☐	☐	☐	☐	____
10. scrub and dry my feet completely	☐	☐	☐	☐	____
11. shave myself	☐	☐	☐	☐	____
12. take a bath	☐	☐	☐	☐	____
13. throw away the garbage	☐	☐	☐	☐	____
14. use cologne	☐	☐	☐	☐	____
15. use deodorant	☐	☐	☐	☐	____
16. wash my clothes	☐	☐	☐	☐	____
17. wash my hair using soap or mild shampoo	☐	☐	☐	☐	____

    ◆ I should always ...

	True	False
a) wash my hands after using the toilet.	☐	☐
b) wash my hands before making or eating food.	☐	☐
c) wash my hands after handling dogs or other animals.	☐	☐
d) wash my hands if I have been around someone who has a cold.	☐	☐

Topic 8: Sharing Reminiscences

Exercise 1: First Memories

Purpose:

    A. To use reminiscences in order to raise levels of self-esteem.
    B. To discuss first positive memories.

Hints and Procedures:

Warm up the group discussion with the traditional saying "recalling is living" as related to reminiscences. Distribute the handouts provided below. Encourage the members to share their positive first memories and feelings related to them.

Group Session Model:

The objective of this group session was to reinforce the use of reminiscence in order to raise levels of self-esteem. The participants were given handouts with questions to be answered related to their first positive memories. The group discussion focused on the positive feelings evoked by the first positive memories. The clinician facilitated the group discussion on the use of reminiscence and prompted the members to answer questions related to this topic.

The patient came to the group session neat and clean, but seemed depressed and anxious at times. The patient was observed as being isolated and having a sad facial expression and a rigid posture. However, the patient was able to relate to his peers and responded appropriately to the questions. The patient shared with the members his first and favorite vacation by stating, "My first vacation was at a beach in Cuba. I was a little boy, and it was the first time that I stayed at a beach. It was a very exciting and enjoyable experience in my life. Talking about such a memory makes me feel so good."

Positive reinforcement was provided by the members regarding the patient's positive memory, to which he was receptive.

The professional team has recommended that the patient will need this level of service in order to continue working on raising his level of self-esteem in an effort to combat his mental illness symptoms and stabilize his mood.

Topic 8: Sharing Reminiscences

Exercise 1: First Memories

My First Positive Memories

The use of reminiscence may be an enjoyable activity for the majority of people. Regardless of any background or negative experience, it is possible to have good and positive memories from our past. Remembering such memories brings us positive feelings and can help us raise our levels of self-esteem.

- Please answer the following questions:

  ✧ What has been one of your first positive memories?

  1. My first favorite toy was _____
  2. My first favorite holiday tradition was _____
  3. My first favorite place to live was _____
  4. My first favorite town/city was _____
  5. My first favorite teacher was _____
  6. My first favorite vacation was _____
  7. My first favorite job was _____
  8. My first best friend was _____
  9. My first best school was _____
  10. My first best success was _____

  ✧ Why was that your favorite memory?

  ✧ What are your feelings related to the above memory?

Topic 8: Sharing Reminiscences

Exercise 2: Family Memories

Purpose:

    A. To identify and revive positive family memories.

Hints and Procedures:

Distribute the handouts provided below, and encourage the members to answer the questions related to their positive family memories. Promote the group discussion by using the content of each question related to the members' positive family memories. Provide the members with feedback for the positive feelings evoked from the positive memories.

Group Session Model:

The group session's objective was a discussion of reminiscing. The discussion focused on positive family memories. In order to facilitate the group activity, the members were encouraged to use handouts containing information and several questions related to family memories. The group discussion focused on the importance of reviving positive memories from family experiences as a way to increase feelings of pride and raise levels of self-esteem.

The patient appeared depressed as evidenced by a low energy level, sadness, and isolation. The patient was responsive under minimum prompting and recalled a positive message of his family by stating, "I always have learned from my family that politeness works in any part of this world. That is why I try to be a polite person."

Positive feedback was provided by the members regarding the patient's politeness. The patient responded positively to the feedback received and reported benefits from the group session.

The staff has determined that the patient continues to be in need of receiving treatment to increase his level of self-esteem and reduce signs of his depression to a more manageable level.

Topic 8: Sharing Reminiscences

Exercise 2: Family Memories

REMENBERING MY FAMILY

Reviving positive memories and positive messages from our families may be an excellent way to help us bring about nice feelings and increase our levels of self-esteem. This activity today will help you to achieve this task.

- All about your family memories:

    1. What kind of positive messages were given to you about **family values**?
    2. What kind of positive messages were given to you about **children**?
    3. What kind of positive messages were given to you about **spiritual life**?
    4. What kind of positive messages were given to you about **social life**?
    5. What kind of positive messages were given to you about **professional life**?
    6. What kind of positive messages were given to you about **work**?
    7. What kind of positive messages were given to you about **cleanliness**?
    8. What kind of positive messages were given to you about **play**?
    9. Which people in your family have played important parts in your life?
    10. How were people in your family in touch with each other?

Topic 8: Sharing Reminiscences

Exercise 3: Sunday Memories

Purpose:

    A. To revive positive Sunday memories.
    B. To share memories and compare experiences.

Hints and Procedures:

While the handouts are being passed out, introduce the topic with the old saying *"recalling is living."* Encourage the members to revive their positive Sunday memories. Discuss the benefits of sharing positive memories. Focus the group discussion on the positive feelings related to the memories.

Group Session Model:

This group session was on reminiscing. The clinician warmed up the group discussion by reviewing the old saying "recalling is living." The members were provided with handouts with questions about Sunday memories and were encouraged to revive them by answering the questions. The group discussion focused on the benefits of sharing positive memories including the positive feelings related to them.

The patient has regularly displayed a dominant depressive mental status interfering with his daily level of functioning. Some of the patient's symptoms remain similar to the previous sessions, including sadness, agitation, and initial isolation. The patient was responsive to minimum prompting and was able to share with his peers a very enjoyable activity he used to do on Sundays with his family when he was a child. The patient stated, "Every Sunday, my father and my mother used to take me to church. It was very enjoyable to sit together with many kids in our church and learn about the Bible written for kids."

Positive feedback and support were provided by the members regarding the patient's positive memories. The patient responded positively to the feedback and indicated his understanding of the concepts of reminiscing discussed during the group discussion.

The staff will continue working on raising the patient's level of self-esteem using reminiscence and other strategies as part of his stabilization process.

Topic 8: Sharing Reminiscences

Exercise 3: Sunday Memories

My Sunday's Positive Memories

It is always enjoyable to share with others our positive memories. It is like the old saying that "recalling is living." Therefore, why not go back a little bit to our pasts today and recall some of those beautiful and positive Sunday memories? However, please, recall only positive memories!

- Please answer the following questions:

    ◆ Do you recall what Sundays were like in your house growing up?

    1. Did you used to spend time with your family?
    2. Did you used to go for rides?
    3. Did you used to go church? How was your experience?
    4. Did you used to dress in your Sunday best? How was that?
    5. Did you used to slick your hair?
    6. Did you used to brush your teeth?
    7. Was there any special cooking? Which kind?
    8. What did you used to eat for lunch?
    9. How did you used to go out? By horses? By car?
    10. What did you used to like doing most on your Sundays?

    ◆ Tell us one of your best positive Sunday memories:

Topic 8: Sharing Reminiscences

Exercise 4: Romantic Memories

Purpose:

    A. To practice reminiscence by reviving romantic memories.
    B. To raise levels of self-esteem by increasing self-acceptance.

Hints and Procedures:

Review with the members the Valentine's Day tradition. Recall memories of the first Valentine's Day cards, flowers, and gifts they sent or received. Tell the members about this tradition. The first known Valentine's Day card was sent from the Tower of London by a French prisoner to his wife in 1415. In 1988, 900 million Valentine's Day cards were sent in the US. Encourage the members to answer the questions from the handouts about other romantic memories and promote the group discussion about the positive feelings associated with them.

Group Session Model:

The group session focused on practicing reminiscence by reviving romantic memories. The clinician warmed up the group discussion by briefly reviewing the Valentine's Day tradition. Then the members were encouraged to answer questions from handouts related to positive romantic memories. The group discussion focused on the positive feelings elicited by the romantic memories.

The patient has regularly indicated depression with psychotic features. He was observed with an avoidant affect and paranoid mood. He was isolated, had slouched shoulders, and was impulsive for a brief period, leaving the room abruptly without asking for permission from the clinician. Despite being redirected and encouraged to participate, the patient was somewhat reluctant to fully contribute in a spontaneous manner. He answered only one question from the handout by adding, "My most romantic moment in my life was when I had my first date."

The members praised the patient for that romantic moment, to which the patient was receptive.

The future sessions will continue to stimulate the patient to practice reminiscence, promote expression of positive feelings, and raise his level of self-esteem.

Topic 8: Sharing Reminiscences

Exercise 4: Romantic Memories

Practicing reminiscence is an enjoyable activity and a way to strengthen identity and raise levels of self-esteem. It can be funny to revive and talk about those romantic memories from our pasts.

- Try to answer some of the questions below so you can share with your peers some of your romantic memories.

    1. How was your first kiss? How did you feel?
    2. Who was your first love? What was the person like? Where is that person now?
    3. Who was the most romantic person that you have met? Why?
    4. When did you celebrate your first Valentine's Day? How was that?
    5. What gift did you buy for your partner? How did your partner feel?
    6. What gift did you receive? How did you feel?
    7. Have you ever sent a love poem? To whom?
    8. Have you ever written a poem? If yes, can you recite some lines?
    9. What love song do you recall? Can you sing a little bit?
    10. What was your most romantic memory? Why?
    11. What was your most romantic movie? Why?
    12. What was your most romantic book? Why?

Topic 8: Sharing Reminiscences

Exercise 5: Memorable Periods

Purpose:

A. To relive positive periods in life and associated feelings.

Hints and Procedures:

While the handouts are being distributed, review the concepts of "sense of well-being" and "self-esteem" as a warming-up activity. Encourage the members to choose positive periods in their lives and describe any associated feelings related to them, as well as the impact they have had on their lives.

Group Session Model:

The group session focused on encouraging the members to relive positive periods in their lives in order to support a sense of well-being and raise their levels of self-esteem. The members were provided with handouts with a list of several possible memorable and positive periods in a person's life. Then they were encouraged to describe any associated feelings related to those memorable moments as well as the impact they have had on their lives.

The patient's depressed mood and affect persisted during the session. He showed a sad facial expression, and was self-absorbed and withdrawn in the group today. Upon being prompted and encouraged, the patient stated, "A memorable experience in my life was during my childhood. I was a happy child living with both parents. I feel proud of belonging to my current family who has been providing me with love and support despite being mentally ill."

Positive reinforcement was provided by the members to support the patient's memorable experience. The patient was receptive to the feedback received and recognized the benefits of using reminiscence of memorable experiences to raise his level of self-esteem.

The professional team has suggested the patient's continued attendance to this level of service in order to raise his level of self-esteem, decrease his psychiatric symptoms, and prevent hospitalization.

Topic 8: Sharing Reminiscences

Exercise 5: Memorable Periods

A Positive Period in my Life

We all may have at least a period in our lives that we would like to relive. It may be a memorable event or experience. It can have a significant impact on our lives and brings us many positive feelings. They may include feelings of pride, belonging, self-worth, self-accomplishment, joy, happiness, hope, well-being, and competence.

- **Choose a positive period in your life below that you would like to relive.**

    A memorable and positive period from my past was ...

    1. during my childhood.
    2. during my adolescence.
    3. during my days in school.
    4. during the time I was dating.
    5. during my wedding ceremony.
    6. during my pregnancy.
    7. during the time when I was living in a foreign country.
    8. during the time when I was learning how to speak another language.
    9. when my first child was born.
    10. when I graduated from high school/college/university.

    ✦ Can you describe your experience above?

    ✦ What feelings has this experience brought into your life?

Topic 8: Sharing Reminiscences

Exercise 6: Highest Point in Life

Purpose:

    A. To use reminiscence to increase levels of self-esteem.
    B. To share positive memories and compare experiences.

Hints and Procedures:

Distribute the handouts provided below. Assist the members in identifying their high points in life, and promote the group discussion on the impact of the positive memories on their present lives. Encourage the members to compare their experiences with each other's.

Group Session Model:

This group session was on reminiscence. The clinician initiated the group discussion by reviewing the use of reminiscence as a learning experience that can help increase levels of self-esteem. The members were asked to identify their high points in life. The group discussion focused on the positive impact of the positive memories on the patients' present lives.

The patient came to the group session neat and clean but seemed depressed and sad. The patient was observed as guarded and isolated from the members. However, the patient was receptive to minimal prompting and was able to complete the group task. The patient expressed himself by stating, "My highest point in life was when I got married. It was a very special moment in my life, and I think for everybody, it is a very unforgettable memory."

The members added validity to the patient's positive memory. The patient was receptive to the group support. Also, the patient was receptive to the idea of continuing to use reminiscence of positive memories in the process of building up a high level of self-esteem.

The staff will continue to encourage the patient to use effective strategies to increase his level of self-esteem as part of the process to help him reach mood stabilization.

Topic 8: Sharing Reminiscences

Exercise 6: Highest Point in Life

The use of recollection can be an enjoyable learning experience in life. Sharing positive memories and comparing experiences with your peers will help you increase your level of self-esteem.

- Try to complete one of the statements below. We will help you complete this task by providing you with some ideas.

    My highest point in life was …

    1. when I graduated from high school.
    2. when I graduated from college.
    3. when I graduated from university.
    4. when I started working.
    5. when I bought my first bicycle.
    6. when I bought my first car.
    7. when I got married.
    8. when I bought my first house.
    9. when my first child was born.
    10. when _____

PART IV

GROUP DEPRESSION

TOPICS 1–4

WITH

THIRTEEN EXERCISES

Topic 1: Learning About Depression

Exercise 1: Depressive Illness

Purpose:

    A. To understand depressive illness.

Hints and Procedures:

    Distribute the handouts provided below. Warm up the group discussion with the text information about increasing knowledge regarding depression. Encourage the members to identify their depressive symptoms related to the three most common types of depression (refer to key answer 2 from the handout). Promote the group discussion by using the content of each question related to depression.

Group Session Model:

    The group session was aimed at helping the members to understand the illness of depression. The clinician educated the members on how increasing knowledge about depression can help them understand symptoms and better cope with them. In order to facilitate the group discussion, the members were given handouts with questions related to the depressive illness. The group discussion focused on the content of each question.

    During the session, the patient was alert, but was observed as sad, and sat back quietly. He participated only when directly approached. The patient stated, "I know that depression is not my fault. It does not mean that I am weak or lazy. It means that I need help to get myself stable again."

    The patient's opinion was supported by the members. During the course of the group discussion, the patient gained further knowledge of the illness of depression including definitions of depression, types of depression, and the key for treatment of depression. He seemed receptive to the group discussion and support.

    The future sessions will continue to provide the patient with opportunities to apply the knowledge about the illness of depression discussed in order to decrease its symptoms.

Topic 1: Learning About Depression

Exercise 1: Depressive Illness

Increasing knowledge about depression can help you understand its symptoms and be able to cope with them more effectively. Therefore, today this group session is going to be all about the depressive illness. Let's see how much you know about this common mental illness in our modern world.

- Are you ready to start? But, please, do not cry, okay?[1]

    1. What is depression?
    2. What are the three common types of depression?
    3. What do you know about each one?
    4. What are the three levels of depression? Which one is more severe? Why?
    5. Can depression be cured? Why? When?
    6. What can help you understand symptoms of depression?
    7. Who is at fault for your depression?
    8. What can you do with your depression? What is the key?
    9. What are the available treatments for depression?
    10. Where do you go for help for your depression?

---

[1] Answer key:
  1. Depression is a medical disorder, just like high blood pressure, stomach ulcers, and heart disease.
  2. The three common types of depression are major depression, dysthymia, and bipolar disorder.
  3. Major depression begins suddenly, is severe, and continues for months or years; dysthymia has symptoms that are not as severe as those of major depression are, but may last for years; bipolar disorder includes ups and downs with sudden changes of mood and symptoms of mania.
  4. The levels of depression are mild, moderate, and severe.
  5. Depression can be cured when it is not originated from a primary mental illness or when it is the source of an environmental situation.
  6. Increasing knowledge about depression can help in understanding its symptoms.
  7. Nobody should be blamed for being depressed.
  8. The sooner treatment begins, the faster the recovery.

Topic 1: Learning About Depression

Exercise 2: Depressive Effects

Purpose:

    A. To promote group discussion about depressive effects.

Hints and Procedures:

    Provide the members with the handouts, and initiate the group discussion by using the first three questions about depressive effects. Continue the group discussion with the remaining questions.

Group Session Model:

    The group session was developed to discuss with the members the depressive effects. The members were given handouts with questions related to the depressive effects. The group discussion focused on how depression affects people's thoughts, feelings, behaviors, bodies, and social and spiritual lives, as well as how depression has affected the members.

    Prior to the session, the patient was depressed. The patient sat apart from his peers with a sad facial expression and downcast eyes, and seemed somewhat anxious. However, the patient had no difficulty sharing with the members how depression has affected his behaviors as evidenced in his statement: "My depression has affected my behavior. I used to be a very active person before, and when I became depressed, I isolated myself too much. Now, I do not want to do anything."

    The therapeutic intervention consisted of providing the members with clarification, reassurance, and positive unconditional regard. The patient responded positively to the therapeutic intervention.

    The professional team will continue to assist and encourage the patient to learn more about his depressive mental illness as an important step in the development of combined treatments to cope with its related symptoms.

Topic 1: Learning About Depression

Exercise 2: Depressive Effects

Today, we are going to talk about the depressive effects. Knowing about the influence of depression among people will help you learn more about this common disease in our modern society.

- Choose one of the questions below that you would like to discuss with your peers.

    1. Who does depression affect?[1]
    2. When does depression affect people?[2]
    3. Who has a higher risk to become depressed?[3] Why?
    4. How does depression affect a person's thoughts?
    5. How does depression affect a person's feelings?
    6. How does depression affect a person's behaviors?
    7. How does depression affect a person's body?
    8. How does depression affect a person's social life?
    9. How does depression affect a person's spiritual life?
    10. How has depression affected you?

---

[1] Depression can affect anyone. It affects people of all races and ages, and all social, economic, and educational backgrounds. It affects the elderly, middle-aged adults, young adults, teenagers, children, married people, and women.

[2] Depression affects people at any time.

[3] Women, teenagers, and the elderly have a higher risk of depression.

Topic 1: Learning About Depression

Exercise 3: Depressive Impacts

Purpose:

    A. To discuss the impact of depression on five life dimensions.

Hints and Procedures:

    Distribute the handouts provided below, and warm up the group discussion by reviewing the following five life dimensions: physical, emotional, social, intellectual, and spiritual. Encourage the group discussion about the negative impacts of depression on these five life dimensions.

Group Session Model:

    The group session consisted of encouraging the members to discuss the impact of depression on the following five life dimensions: physical, emotional, social, intellectual, and spiritual. The clinician facilitated the group discussion by assisting the members in identifying the negative impacts of depression related to these five life dimensions.

    The patient displayed affects of depression during the session, which included sadness, withdrawal, and lethargy. When approached directly, the patient responded softly. The patient shared with his peers the impact of his depression on his emotional life dimension by commenting, "Now that I am depressed, I feel sad every day, and I cry very often."

    The members added validity to the patient's feeling and behavior. The patient expressed gratitude for the support received. The patient benefited from this group session by learning the negative impact of depression on his life.

    The staff has recommended that the patient continue to be assisted with further therapeutic approaches in order to learn other principles of depression and apply them toward his stabilization process.

Topic 1: Learning About Depression

Exercise 3: Depressive Impacts

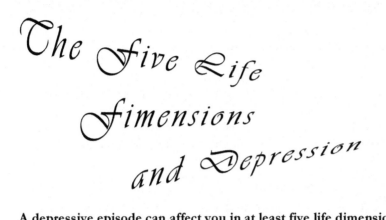

A depressive episode can affect you in at least five life dimensions as follows: physical, emotional, social, intellectual, and spiritual. Learning the impact of this disease on these five life dimensions will help you better understand this mental illness. So, let's test your knowledge!

- Please identify at least two negative impacts of depression on the following:[1]

    ◆ Physical life: _____

    ◆ Emotional life: _____

    ◆ Social life: _____

    ◆ Intellectual life: _____

    ◆ Spiritual life: _____

---

[1] Answer key:
Physical may include low energy level, fatigue, tiredness, psychomotor retardation or agitation, and decreased metabolism.
Emotional may include feelings of sadness, crying episodes, anger, helplessness, hopelessness, guilt, and self-punishment.
Social may include isolation, dependence, manipulative and withdrawal behaviors, poor support system, and disappointments.
Intellectual may include development of irrational thoughts, difficulty concentrating, negative outlook about self and the future, negativism toward all life dimensions, and excessive use of defensive mechanisms such as minimization, denial, rationalization, and personalization.
Spiritual may include feelings of worthlessness and lack of personal values, lack of purpose and meaning in life, resistance to feeling pleasure, feelings of guilt, and misconceptions.

Topic 1: Learning About Depression

Exercise 4: Stages of Depression

Purpose:

    A. To identify and discuss the six stages of depression.

Hints and Procedures:

    Distribute the handouts provided below. Promote the group discussion on each of the six stages of depression. Assist the members in recognizing and identifying the severity of each stage of depression and which stage they are going through.

Group Session Model:

    The purpose of this group session was to encourage the members to identify and discuss the six stages of depression. In order to facilitate the group discussion, the members were asked to use handouts with information about the symptoms of the six stages of depression. Also, explanations of how to recognize the severity of each stage of depression were provided.

    During the session, the patient presented to the group as depressed, evidenced by a flat affect and a very sad mood. The patient sat erect and was opening and closing his eyes. On approach and upon prompting, the patient commented on the feelings stage of depression as follows: "Most of the times I have a feeling of emptiness, I do not understand myself, and I feel confused."

    The therapeutic intervention consisted of providing the members with reassurance, support, and, furthermore, with cognitive behavioral education aimed at helping the members learn about the six stages of depression. The patient was receptive to the intervention provided.

    The staff will continue to assist the patient with therapeutic interventions aimed at decreasing his depressive symptoms and reaching his mood stabilization.

Topic 1: Learning About Depression

Exercise 4: Stages of Depression

The Six Stages of Depression

Learning about the stages of depression and their corresponding symptoms will help you think about combined treatments that you can use to decrease the symptoms and get yourself stable.

- Please match the symptoms of depressive stages in the first column with the stages of depression in the second column.[1]

  Symptoms of Depressive Stages

  1. (   ) Feelings of emptiness and confusion
  2. (   ) Giving up hopes and goals
  3. (   ) Needs, thoughts, or feelings are not expressed
  4. (   ) Expression of hopes and goals are stopped
  5. (   ) Hope is lost
  6. (   ) Sense of identity is lost

  Stages

  (a) The Silence
  (b) The Identity
  (c) The Feelings
  (d) The Loss
  (e) The Stagnation
  (f) The Giving up

  ✧ Which stage of depression are you at present?

  ✧ What stage of depression above do you think is the most severe? Why?

---

[1] Answer key: 1 (c); 2 (f); 3 (a); 4 (e); 5 (d); 6 (b).

Topic 2: Identifying Sources of Depression

Exercise 1: Causes of Depression

Purpose:

    A. To identify and discuss causes of depression.

Hints and Procedures:

    Distribute the handouts provided below. Warm up the group discussion by asking the members the question, "Is depression your fault?" Encourage the members to identify the causes of their depression. Promote the group discussion with the content of each statement related to causes of depression.

Group Session Model:

    The group session was designed to identify and discuss causes of depression. In order to facilitate the group discussion, the members were given handouts with several true-or-false statements related to possible causes of depression. The group discussion focused on the important information associated with the causes of depression.

    The patient appeared with halting speech, constant fidgeting, and a predominant anxious affect. The patient stated, "I think that the cause of my depression runs in my family, because my mother was a very depressed person."

    The patient was informed that it is possible that a tendency for depression can be in part genetic, lending support to his opinion. The patient was receptive to the support received. Also, he had an opportunity to learn about many other causes of depression that in a direct or indirect way may apply to him as well.

    The staff has recommended the patient's continuous attendance to this level of service in order to work on decreasing his depressive symptoms and reaching mood stabilization.

84 ■ *Group Depression*

Topic 2: Identifying Sources of Depression

Exercise 1: Causes of Depression

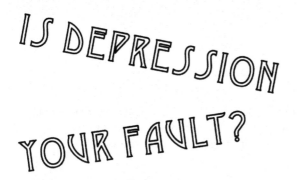
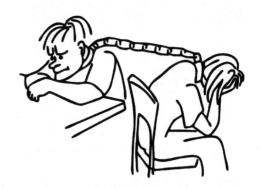

Depression is not your fault. It does not mean that you are weak or lazy. It means that you need help. So, what can be the causes of depression?[1] Experts are not exactly sure, but one or more of the causes below may apply to you.

- Which statements below are true (T) or false (F)?[2]

	Statement	T or F?
1.	Depression can be inherited and tends to run in families.	( )
2.	Biochemical tendencies cannot be genetic.	( )
3.	Hormonal changes are more related to women in postpartum depression.	( )
4.	Alcohol or drug abuse cannot affect the brain's natural chemical production.	( )
5.	Brain chemistry imbalance plays a role in some cases of depression.	( )
6.	Financial problems are a type of loss that can lead only to a mild depression.	( )
7.	Depression may develop soon after the death of a loved one.	( )
8.	Depression does not occur around the anniversary of a death event.	( )
9.	Conflict with family can trigger a depressive episode.	( )
10.	Demanding and extroverted people are more prone to develop depression.	( )
11.	Some medications may cause a low mood and fatigue similar to depression.	( )
12.	Physical illness would never be a cause of depression.	( )
13.	Legal issues are one of the most common causes of depression.	( )
14.	Environmental influences may lead to stress but not to depression.	( )

✧ Why do you think the statements above are true or false?

---

[1] They may include genetic and hereditary factors, hormonal changes, financial problems, environmental influences, and legal issues. In addition, other causes include brain chemistry, the death of a family member, and conflict with family, personality type, medication, physical illness, and alcohol and drug abuse.

[2] Answer key: 1) True, 2) False, 3) True, 4) False, 5) True, 6) False, 7) True, 8) False, 9) True, 10) False, 11) True, 12) False, 13) True, 14) False.

Topic 2: Identifying Sources of Depression

Exercise 2: Factors of Depression

Purpose:

    A. To recognize factors contributing to depression.
    B. To discuss alternative ways to overcome factors contributing to depression.

Hints and Procedures:

While the handouts are being passed out, warm up the group discussion by introducing the idea that we may have different perceptions about what happens in our lives, such as factors contributing to depression. Some factors may not be the ones that people think have been contributing to their depression. For instance, although drug and alcohol addiction can be considered one of the factors leading to depression, other factors, such as poor coping skills and lack of knowledge, may be the real factors contributing to depression. Encourage the members to come up with alternative ways to overcome the factors contributing to their depression.

Group Session Model:

This group session consisted of assisting the members in recognizing factors contributing to their depression. The members were given handouts with a list of factors that directly or indirectly may contribute to depression. The members were encouraged to choose the factors that could be contributing to their depression as well as discuss alternative ways to overcome them.

Although at the beginning of the session, the patient was observed as sad, indicating a moderate sign of depression, he came to the group session attentive, animated, and involved in the group discussion with minimal prompting. The patient stated, "For me, I think lack of knowledge was one of the factors that contributed to my depression. If I had learned before what I have learned here now, I probably would not have become so depressed."

The therapeutic intervention consisted of providing the members with positive feedback, moral support, and reassurance. The patient was receptive to the therapeutic intervention. Also, the patient demonstrated greater insight into many other factors contributing to depression as were discussed by the members.

Continued group psychotherapy sessions are recommended for this patient in order to monitor his progress, offer him support, decrease his depressive symptoms, and stabilize his mood.

Topic 2: Identifying Sources of Depression

Exercise 2: Factors of Depression

There are many factors that can contribute to depression. They may be direct or indirect, you may be aware or not aware of them, and they may not be exactly what you think they are. Recognizing and understanding the factors contributing to your depression may help you to decrease your depressive episodes.

- Please complete the two statements below:

  ✧ One factor contributing to my depression is/was my ...

  1. Excessive isolation
  2. Poor coping skills
  3. Lack of knowledge
  4. Lack of a consistent direction
  5. Lack of discipline
  6. Drug/alcohol addiction
  7. Difficulty concentrating
  8. Poor insight
  9. Poor support system
  10. Lack of commitment
  11. Lack of persistence
  12. Lack of freedom
  13. Aging process
  14. Other _____

  ✧ One alternative way to overcome this factor is _____

Topic 3: Identifying Symptoms of Depression

Exercise 1: Individual Symptoms

Purpose:

A. To identify and recognize individual symptoms of depression.

Hints and Procedures:

While the handouts are being distributed, review some concepts related to depression, including its definition and its effects on a person as a whole. Use the list of depressive symptoms and statements related to depression to help the members identity their symptoms and facilitate the group discussion. Reinforce any symptom relief, and encourage the members to come up with ideas on how to feel better in the future.

Group Session Model:

This group session's objective was to help the members identify and recognize individual symptoms of depression. The members were given handouts with a list of several symptoms of depression and were asked to identity their symptoms from the list. The group discussion focused on symptom relief they have been experiencing and what to do to keep feeling better in the future.

The patient under treatment in the session was observed as suspicious, with a flat facial expression, and guarded. The patient had poor eye contact and was talking to himself most of the time. Also, he needed encouragement to participate in the group discussion. When prompted, the patient stated, "The most common symptoms of my depression have been my sleeping problem. I take my sleeping pill every day, but I still cannot sleep well."

The patient was encouraged to further elaborate on what to do with his symptoms. The patient received support and encouragement from his peers, including motivation and suggestions on how to continue feeling better in the future. The patient seemed receptive to the support, encouragement, and motivation received.

The plan for the future sessions is to continue to encourage the patient to apply the concepts and suggestions provided during the group sessions.

Topic 3: Identifying Symptoms of Depression

Exercise 1: Individual Symptoms

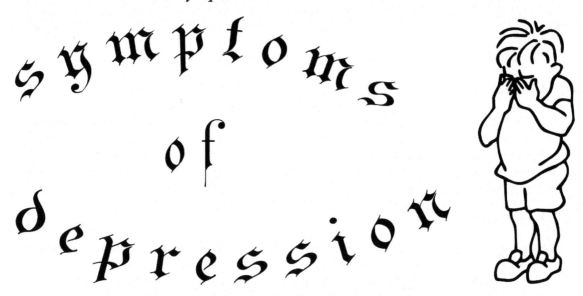

Depression is a mood disorder that affects the whole person—body, mind, and spirit. There is a broad range of symptoms of depression that you may have been experiencing. Identifying them should be one of the first steps in your process of treating your depression. So, let's help you to do that today.

- Please complete the three parts below:

    Part I. The most common symptoms of my depression have been ...

    - ( ) 1. Loss of interest
    - ( ) 2. Suicidal ideas
    - ( ) 3. Appetite disturbances
    - ( ) 4. Death wishes
    - ( ) 5. Low level of self-esteem
    - ( ) 6. Anxiety
    - ( ) 7. Isolation
    - ( ) 8. Irritability
    - ( ) 9. Feelings of guilt
    - ( ) 10. Weight loss or gain
    - ( ) 11. Poor hygiene and grooming
    - ( ) 12. Withdrawal from people and activities
    - ( ) 13. Persistent physical symptoms
    - ( ) 14. Sleeping disturbances
    - ( ) 15. Difficulty concentrating
    - ( ) 16. Low energy level and lack of motivation
    - ( ) 17. Feelings of sadness and crying spells
    - ( ) 18. Loss of pleasure and enjoyment of life
    - ( ) 19. Feelings of worthlessness
    - ( ) 20. Feelings of restlessness
    - ( ) 21. Feelings of hopelessness/helplessness
    - ( ) 22. Other _____

    Part II. I have experienced the following symptoms released by
    _____

    Part III. I can keep feeling better in the future by
    _____

Topic 3: Identifying Symptoms of Depression

Exercise 2: Consequences of Depression

Purpose:

A. To discuss the negative consequences of depression in a person's life.

Hints and Procedures:

Initiate the group discussion by reviewing defensive mechanisms (e.g., denial is one of the main defense mechanisms in mental illness issues). Provide the members with the handouts, and challenge each member to identify the negative consequences of depression in their lives. If a patient denies illness, chart it as lack of understanding or lack of insight. If a patient cannot identify any negative consequences of depression in his or her life, ask if he or she knows anyone else who might have experienced them.

Group Session Model:

The subject of this group session was on the negative consequences of depression in people's lives. The clinician initiated the group session by reviewing with the members the defense mechanism of denial as one of the main defense mechanisms in dealing with mental illness issues. The members were provided with handouts with information and questions related to the topic and a list of possible negative consequences of depression in people's lives. The group discussion focused on the content of the material provided.

In the group session, the patient was withdrawn and guarded, had a depressed mood, and displayed little to no affect. On approach and upon being prompted, the patient commented, "Depression has negatively impacted my social life. When I feel depressed, I like to be left alone by myself, and I just like to go into my room, close the door, and lie down."

The clinician discussed with the patient some other consequences of depression in a person's life, including death wishes and death produced by a suicidal action. The patient improved his knowledge of the negative consequences of depression in his own life. He agreed to start developing methods to improve him and prevent further exacerbation of his depressive symptoms.

The group sessions will continue to assist the patient in increasing his knowledge about depression and implementing methods to eliminate or reduce the negative consequences of depression in his life.

Topic 3: Identifying Symptoms of Depression

Exercise 2: Consequences of Depression

What may be the negative consequences of depression in a person's life? In a direct or indirect way, depression may lead to many negative consequences in a person's life. The consequences may be mild, moderate, or severe. Knowing the consequences is a very important step in developing combined treatments to cope with this kind of mental illness. So, let's try to increase your understanding and insight about how depression has been negatively impacting your own life.

- Please answer the following questions:

    A. What could be the worst negative consequence of depression in a person's life?

    B. What if a person denies being depressed? What should be done?

    C. Can you identify one negative consequence of depression in your life below? If not, why?

    1. Social withdrawal
    2. Physical impairment
    3. Psychotic symptoms
    4. Breaking the law
    5. Suicidal ideas
    6. Impaired level of functioning
    7. Drug/alcohol involvement
    8. Imprisonment
    9. Death wishes
    10. Suicide attempt

    D. What should be done with the negative consequences of depression above?

Topic 4: Developing Coping Mechanisms to Cope with Depression

Exercise 1: Treating Depression

Purpose:

A. To explore sources and types of treatment for depression.

Hints and Procedures:

Distribute the handouts provided below to facilitate the group discussion related to treating depression. Use the content of each statement to answer the following three questions: Who are the people that treat depression? Where does one get help for depression? What treatments are available for depression? Discuss with the members the main objective of each treatment for depression.

Group Session Model:

This group session was developed to explore sources and types of treatment for depression. In order to facilitate the group discussion, the members were given handouts with true-or-false statements related to treatments for depression. The content of the statements focused on the three following questions: Who are the people that treat depression? Where does one get help? What treatments are available for depression? The group discussion centered on the main objective of each treatment, including psychotherapies and medications.

The patient has frequently exhibited a dominant depressive mental status interfering with his daily functional level. Among them, the patient was observed as guarded, with downcast eyes, poor insight, and detachment. When prompted by the clinician to share with the members any information related to the topic, he added, "I have learned that cognitive therapy can help me to change my negative way of thinking, my conduct, and my mood."

The patient's opinion was supported by the members and with other approaches discussed. The patient responded positively to feedback and was receptive to the new information learned.

Based on the patient's current depressive mental status, it is recommended that the patient continue to attend this level of service in order to decrease his symptoms of depression and stabilize his mood.

Topic 4: Developing Coping Mechanisms to Cope with Depression

Exercise 1: Treating Depression

There are many sources of help and types of treatment for depression available in our community. Knowing people who treat depression, where to get help, and the types of treatment available for depression is a very important step to treat this kind of mental illness. Completing the true-or-false statements below will help you to learn more about this important subject.

- Which statements below are true (T) or false (F)?[1]

    ( ) 1. Psychiatrists are medical doctors who can diagnose illness and prescribe medication.
    ( ) 2. Psychotherapists and counselors treat depression and prescribe medication.
    ( ) 3. Psychologists test, diagnose, and treat psychological disturbances.
    ( ) 4. Psychiatric nurses and social workers, but not clergy members, can treat depression.
    ( ) 5. Psychoanalysts use a special talking out form of therapy for deeply rooted problems.
    ( ) 6. Schools and large employers are the best place to get treatment for depression.
    ( ) 7. Mental health centers and mental hospitals have specialized treatment for depression.
    ( ) 8. General hospitals and family service agencies do not offer treatment for depression.
    ( ) 9. Treatment for depression can be found in self-help groups and suicide prevention hotlines.
    ( ) 10. Medication might be the only effective way to treat depression.
    ( ) 11. Medication and psychotherapy are the most effective treatments for depression.
    ( ) 12. Common types of psychotherapies include cognitive and interpersonal, but not psychodynamic.

---

[1] Answer key: 1) True, 2) False, 3) True, 4) False, 5) True, 6) False, 7) True, 8) False, 9) True, 10) False, 11) True, 12) False.

Topic 4: Developing Coping Mechanisms to Cope with Depression

Exercise 2: Identifying Strategies

Purpose:

    A. To develop strategies to cope with depression.
    B. To identify activities to cope with depression.

Hints and Procedures:

Distribute the handouts provided below. Encourage the members to identify activities they want to become involved in. Promote the group discussion on how to become involved in the activities to cope with depression, including strategies and the frequency of each activity. Discuss the importance of making a commitment to become consistently involved in the activities discussed.

Group Session Model:

This group session consisted of encouraging the members to develop strategies to cope with depression. In order to facilitate the group activity, the members were given handouts containing a list of several activities to cope with depression. The members were asked to choose the activities they wanted to become involved in. The group discussion focused on the importance of making a commitment to become consistently involved in the activities discussed.

During the session, the patient showed classic signs of depression—a sad facial expression and isolated and guarded behaviors. However, the patient was responsive to moderate prompting, attentive, cooperative, and receptive to suggestions. The patient focused on his spiritual beliefs, so he selected a daily activity from the handout on this basis. The patient told the group, "Since I am a spiritually oriented person, from now on, I want to read the Bible every day."

The therapeutic means consisted of providing the members with psychotherapeutic education, encouragement, guidance, and positive feedback. The patient was receptive to the therapeutic intervention. Also, he agreed to implement in the future other strategies discussed during the group discussion.

Continued psychotherapy is recommended for this patient to monitor his progress, and offer him support and reinforcement to decrease his depressive symptoms and stabilize his mood.

Topic 4: Developing Coping Mechanisms to Cope With Depression

Exercise 2: Identifying Strategies

My way out of depression

A person who is experiencing depression may spend a whole day or many days lying in bed and doing nothing. If a person is in a state of severe depression, what can be done? The first step would be to identify strategies to cope with the depressive symptoms. Strategies, such as activities to get involved in, can help break the cycle of such severe depressive mood status and help the person to feel better.

- Please, answer the three following questions:

    ◆ Can you identify at least three of your favorite activities below?

    1. Arranging to be with people
    2. Complying with my medication
    3. Gardening
    4. Getting up early in the morning
    5. Keeping myself busy
    6. Meditating
    7. Playing cards
    8. Reaching out to someone
    9. Recalling good times
    10. Replacing negative thoughts
    11. Spending time with a close friend
    12. Watching TV
    13. Being good to myself
    14. Exercising
    15. Getting in touch with my higher power
    16. Implementing the twelve-step program
    17. Laughing
    18. Participating in a support group
    19. Praying
    20. Reading
    21. Refusing to feel guilty
    22. Resting
    23. Spending time with my children
    24. Working on meeting my needs

    ◆ What do you need to do to become involved in these activities?

    ◆ How often should you become involved in these activities?

Topic 4: Developing Coping Mechanisms to Cope with Depression

Exercise 3: Overcoming Depression

Purpose:

    A. To use the twelve steps to overcome depression.

Hints and Procedures:

    Provide the members with the handouts, and promote the group discussion by using the twelve steps to overcome depression. Assist and encourage the members to identify which step they want to start working on and encourage them to take immediate action. Promote the group discussion with the content of each step to overcome depression.

Group Session Model:

    The purpose of this group session was to train the members in the use of the twelve steps to overcome depression. The members were given handouts with the twelve steps to overcome depression. The group session started with a brief review of some negative thoughts and feelings associated with depression. The members were encouraged to identify which steps they wanted to start working on.

    Recently, the patient has been depressed. The patient was observed as sad, somewhat guarded, and isolated from the members. In response to the topic discussed and upon prompting, the patient selected one of the steps and commented, "I want to develop goals to help me sleep better. I want to start walking and practicing relaxation every day."

    Positive reinforcement was provided by the members related to the patient's selected step. The patient was receptive to the reinforcement and agreed to continue working on other steps to overcome his depression.

    The future sessions will continue to assist and encourage the patient to complete the twelve steps to overcome depression and stabilize his mood.

Topic 4: Developing Coping Mechanisms to Cope with Depression

Exercise 3: Overcoming Depression

Depression makes people feel exhausted, worthless, helpless, and hopeless. Negative thoughts and feelings make you feel like giving up. But, you do not have to fight depression on your own. For instance, you can join a support group. Support groups give people with depression a chance to share their feelings with others and talk about things that might help them feel better. The twelve steps to overcome depression below will help you make your life run smoother.

- Choose at least one step to overcome depression to discuss with your peers.

    ☐ 1. I will set realistic goals—identify at least two.
    ☐ 2. I will join a support group—identify at least two groups in the community.
    ☐ 3. I will participate in recreational activities—identify at least two.
    ☐ 4. I will exercise regularly—identify one exercise of your preference.
    ☐ 5. I will learn to laugh—identify at least two activities that can make you laugh.
    ☐ 6. I will take care of my personal hygiene—list as many activities as possible.
    ☐ 7. I will try to be around others—identify at least one person to have contact with daily.
    ☐ 8. I will plan a realistic schedule—identify the things that you have to do daily.
    ☐ 9. I will go out with friends—identify one friend you can go out with at least once a week.
    ☐ 10. I will work on improving my sleep quality—identify at least two methods.
    ☐ 11. I will work on decreasing my stress—identify at least two stress reduction techniques.
    ☐ 12. I will take a break at least once a month, such as an evening out, a trip, a visit, etc.

Topic 4: Developing Coping Mechanisms to Cope with Depression

Exercise 4: Fighting Depression

Purpose:

    A. To increase the ability to fight depression.
    B. To increase personal responsibility in fighting depression.

Hints and Procedures:

Warm up the group discussion with the analogy "fighting depression" as in being a powerful and difficulty enemy in a war with depression. Use the two following questions to facilitate the warming-up activity on fighting depression as if in a real battle: How can we prepare for the battle? How can we succeed? Distribute the handouts provided below, and assist the members in answering the questions about fighting depression. Use the content of each question to promote the group discussion.

Group Session Model:

The group session was designed to increase the members' abilities to fight depression. The clinician warmed up the group discussion with the analogy "fighting depression," as in being a powerful and difficulty enemy in a war with depression. Then the members were asked to use handouts and answer questions on how to fight depression as if in a real war.

The patient came to the group session exhibiting symptoms suggesting depression. Among them, the patient was observed as sad, somewhat guarded, isolated, and tired. However, the patient seemed able to follow the group discussion and understand the concept of "fighting depression" as if in a real battle. The patient discussed with his peers some valuable elements of his plan of action to fight depression. The patient stated, "I believe that I need to be active in my plan of action to fight depression. I need to apply everything that I have learned here and be committed to do what I need to do."

Support, encouragement, and new information were provided by the members to each other. The patient was receptive to the support and encouragement received.

The staff has recommended that the patient will continue to require this level of service in order to overcome or manage his depression.

Topic 4: Developing Coping Mechanisms to Cope with Depression

Exercise 4: Fighting Depression

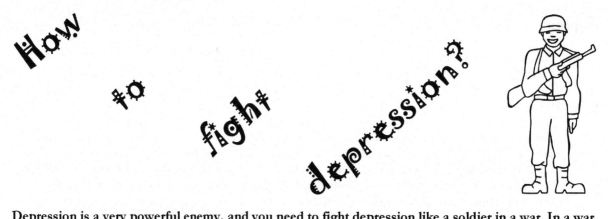

Depression is a very powerful enemy, and you need to fight depression like a soldier in a war. In a war, you need to have effective weapons and receive appropriate training to use them, but you also need to be willing and strong to face your enemy. If you want to beat your depression, you will need to do the same. So, are you going to beat your enemy or hang over?

- **Preparing you for the battle:**[1]

    1. What do you know about your depression? What are your symptoms?
    2. How long is it going to take to win your battle? How can you overcome the hard times?
    3. What weapons (e.g., coping strategies) are you going to need to fight depression?
    4. What is your plan of action to fight depression?
    5. Who is going to support or help you with your battle?
    6. Who is going to be your commandant or guide?
    7. What are other sources of support for your battle?
    8. What predictions can you make about the success of your battle?
    9. Have you been in this battle before?
    10. Which one of your previous learning experiences can you use for the current battle?

    ✧ **Now, let's get in action!**

---

[1] Answer key:
  1. They may include isolation, sleeping problems, crying spells, lack of motivation, anger, anxiety, death wishes, hallucinations, sadness, paranoia, and suicidal ideas.
  2. The fight may be long with good and hard times, and it is necessary to be prepared to overcome the bad days.
  3. It is important to know which weapons (coping strategies) to be used as well as how to use them.
  4. A good plan of action is essential in fighting depression. What should be included in a plan of action?
  5. A good support system should include psychiatrists, counselors, psychotherapists, family members, and peers.
  6. A guideline should be provided by a doctor, including continuous follow-ups with a psychiatrist.
  7. Other sources of support should include social, recreational, and spiritual groups.
  8. What would be the prognosis of "beating the enemy"?
  9. How was that?
  10. Previous learning experiences may be of great help for the current battle.

Topic 4: Developing Coping Mechanisms to Cope with Depression

Exercise 5: Sleeping Disturbance

Purpose:

    A. To develop techniques to improve sleep patterns.
    B. To explore and engage in activities to improve sleep patterns.

Hints and Procedures:

While the handouts are being passed out, ask who in the group suffers from any kind of sleeping disturbances. Warm up the group discussion with the idea of developing healthy sleeping habits to improve the members' quality of sleep. Encourage the members to choose techniques and/or activities to improve their quality of sleep to be practiced on a daily basis. Discuss the benefits of each technique or activity.

Group Session Model:

The group session discussed techniques and activities to improve sleeping patterns. The members were given handouts with a list of several techniques and activities intended to improve their sleeping patterns. The clinician facilitated the group discussion by encouraging the members to implement the techniques and activities to improve their sleeping patterns. Also, the clinician conveyed some of the benefits of using many of the techniques and activities discussed.

The patient reported to the session with a distant affect and paranoid mood. The patient was self-absorbed and isolated from his peers. In response to the topic, the patient stated, "I went for a sleep study test. I have been having problems sleeping for a long time. I take sleep medication daily, but it has not been helping me."

During the course of the group discussion, the patient had an opportunity to explore many activities and techniques to improve his sleeping pattern. Among them, the members discussed the following activities: engagement in physical exercises, relaxation, reading, talking to others to soothe, praying, and listening to music. The patient demonstrated an understanding about the topic discussed as evidenced by a back and forward movement of his head.

The professional team has suggested that the patient will need to continue attending this level of service in order to improve his quality of sleep, improve his level of functioning, and prevent further exacerbation of his psychiatric symptoms.

Topic 4: Developing Coping Mechanisms to Cope with Depression

Exercise 5: Sleeping Disturbance

It is possible for anyone to sleep better by improving his or her sleeping environment. Creating an atmosphere conducive to sleep and using good sleep practices are only a few of the alternatives to improve sleeping pattern. Also, there are many activities that might improve your chances of a good sleep.

- Choose at least two activities to improve your sleep pattern from below. Discuss with your peers their benefits and how to implement these activities.

    ◆ Things that may work for me are:

    ☐ 1. Do physical exercise
    ☐ 2. Listen to music
    ☐ 3. Take a warm bath
    ☐ 4. Pray
    ☐ 5. Take medication
    ☐ 6. Talk to others to soothe
    ☐ 7. Sleep in the same place
    ☐ 8. Wear earplugs
    ☐ 9. Use a nightlight
    ☐ 10. Avoid caffeine
    ☐ 11. Use relaxation techniques
    ☐ 12. Take a walk in the late afternoon
    ☐ 13. Do an unexciting task
    ☐ 14. Read an unexciting book
    ☐ 15. Keep a record of sleeping habits
    ☐ 16. Get up at a set time
    ☐ 17. Use a comfortable cool temperature
    ☐ 18. Follow a set bedtime routine
    ☐ 19. Use a worry time schedule
    ☐ 20. Other _____

    ◆ The benefits of using these activities include
    _____

PART V

GROUP BEHAVIOR

TOPICS 1–4

WITH

TWENTY EXERCISES

Topic 1: Identifying Inappropriate Behaviors

Exercise 1: Triggers and Behaviors

Purpose:

    A. To identify internal and external triggers eliciting inappropriate behaviors.
    B. To explore alternatives to break the cycle of triggers.

Hints and Procedures:

Warm up the group discussion by asking the members for a definition of triggers. Distribute the handout provided below, and use its information to review important concepts related to triggers. Discuss both internal and external triggers. For instance, show examples of how an external trigger can set off an internal one—i.e., how events from the outside world environment can function as external triggers, which may lead to negative feelings (internal triggers).

Group Session Model:

The group session was aimed at encouraging the members to practice the use of internal and external observations of triggers that could elicit inappropriate behaviors. Handouts with information and questions related to internal and external triggers were distributed. The clinician assisted the members in identifying their internal and external triggers. The group discussion focused on triggers eliciting inappropriate behaviors and what to do to avoid them.

During this session, the patient's affect was flat; he had a dysphoric mood and fair eye contact. The patient was somewhat irritated and agitated. In response to the group topic and discussion, the patient stated, "One of my external triggers is money. Whatever I have money in my pocket, it leads me to craving and using drugs."

Although the patient displayed a delayed reaction time to the questions being asked, he seemed able to grasp new information. Also, the patient was receptive to the idea of having his money handled by somebody close to him as an alternative way of avoiding the trigger leading to drug use.

The treatment team has recommended that the patient will need to remain at this level of service to avoid further relapse of his mental illness symptoms or drug addiction.

Topic 1: Identifying Inappropriate Behaviors

Exercise 1: Triggers and Behaviors

Triggers set you off to engage in inappropriate behaviors. They may be internal or external and include thoughts, feelings, people, places, and things. There are two ways to identify your triggers: looking inside yourself and looking outside to the external world. Let's try to practice the internal and external observation so that can help you identify your triggers.

- **Please complete tasks A–D below:**

    ◆ Task A. Which triggers below are internal (I) and which are external (E)?[1]

    ( ) 1. Feelings of fear
    ( ) 2. Feelings of frustration
    ( ) 3. A special song
    ( ) 4. Thoughts of inadequacy
    ( ) 5. Money in my pocket
    ( ) 6. Feelings of sadness
    ( ) 7. A suspicious person
    ( ) 8. Feelings of loneliness
    ( ) 9. Bad news on TV
    ( ) 10. Feelings of hopelessness
    ( ) 11. Somebody drinking or using drugs
    ( ) 12. A picture of somebody dead in my family
    ( ) 13. Feelings of anger
    ( ) 14. Somebody inviting me to get high
    ( ) 15. Thoughts that nobody cares about me
    ( ) 16. A place where I had a bad experience
    ( ) 17. Thoughts that it is okay to use drugs
    ( ) 18. An object that makes me cry
    ( ) 19. Thoughts that I deserve to get high
    ( ) 20. A drug dealer offering free drugs

    ◆ Task B. Choose at least one internal and one external trigger above.

    ◆ Task C. Which inappropriate behaviors can these triggers elicit?

    ◆ Task D. What can you do to break the cycle of the above triggers?

---

[1] Answer key: 1) Internal, 2) Internal, 3) External, 4) Internal, 5) External, 6) Internal, 7) External, 8) Internal, 9) External, 10) Internal, 11) External, 12) External, 13) Internal, 14) External, 15) Internal, 16) External, 17) Internal, 18) External, 19) Internal, 20) External.

Topic 1: Identifying Inappropriate Behaviors

Exercise 2: Undesirable Behaviors

Purpose:

A. To identify and discuss the negative consequences of undesirable behaviors in life.

Hints and Procedures:

After the handouts have been passed out, review some concepts from the learning theories—i.e., good or bad behaviors are learned through our past experiences. Ask the members to identify their undesirable behaviors and make a list of them on the board. Promote a group discussion on the negative consequences of the undesirable behaviors in the mental, social, spiritual, professional, and physiological life dimensions.

Group Session Model:

The group session was developed in order to encourage the members to identify and discuss the negative consequences of undesirable behaviors in their lives. The clinician introduced information that motivated the members to participate and share feelings on the topic. The members were asked to use handouts with a list of several undesirable behaviors. The group discussion focused on the negative consequences of the undesirable behaviors for the following five life dimensions: mental, social, spiritual, professional, and physiological.

In the session, the patient had a depressed mood but with a less anxious affect. The patient had fair eye contact and a well-groomed appearance, and was fully oriented to place, time, and person. On approach, the patient was able to identify and recognize one of his undesirable behaviors. The patient stated, "Suspiciousness has affected my emotional and social life. The last time I became suspicious, I became very agitated and went out of control. As a result, I broke up with my girlfriend and ended up in the hospital."

The patient's behavior was recognized by his peers as undesirable. Also, the patient became aware of many other undesirable behaviors discussed during the group discussion, which in a direct or indirect way may apply to him as well. He seemed receptive to the group discussion.

The professional team has recommended the patient's continuous attendance to this level of service to develop appropriate and functional behaviors supporting his mood stabilization.

Topic 1: Identifying Inappropriate Behaviors

Exercise 2: Undesirable Behaviors

Most of our behaviors are learned through our past experiences. We learn the good, but also the bad or undesirable behaviors as well. The undesirable behaviors can lead to many negative consequences in our mental, social, spiritual, professional, and physiological lives. Probably, your current mental illness may be a product of those past undesirable behaviors in your life. Let's see if one of the behaviors below applies to you.

- Please complete tasks A and B below:

    ◆ Task A. Choose one behavior below which may apply to you:

    ☐ 1. Unresponsiveness
    ☐ 2. Impulsiveness
    ☐ 3. Tardiness
    ☐ 4. Rudeness
    ☐ 5. Restlessness
    ☐ 6. Carelessness
    ☐ 7. Intolerance
    ☐ 8. Obsession
    ☐ 9. Anti-sociality
    ☐ 10. Manipulation
    ☐ 11. Unassertiveness
    ☐ 12. Compulsiveness
    ☐ 13. Aggressiveness
    ☐ 14. Laziness
    ☐ 15. Inattentiveness
    ☐ 16. Suspiciousness
    ☐ 17. Agitation
    ☐ 18. Impatience
    ☐ 19. Attention-seeking behaviors
    ☐ 20. Other _____

    ◆ Task B. What have been the negative consequences of this behavior in your ...

    a) mental life? _____
    b) social life? _____
    c) spiritual life? _____
    d) professional life? _____
    e) physiological life? _____

Topic 1: Identifying Inappropriate Behaviors

Exercise 3: Self-Defeating Behaviors

Purpose:

    A. To discuss the meaning of self-defeating behaviors.
    B. To identify and recognize self-defeating behaviors to prevent self-harm.

Hints and Procedures:

Distribute the handouts provided below, and initiate the group discussion by reading the information related to self-defeating behaviors. Encourage the members to increase awareness of self-defeating behaviors to prevent self-harm. Encourage the members to complete the checklist to identify what self-defeating behaviors they may have been using. Promote the group discussion with these three questions: What do these behaviors say about you? When and why do you use these behaviors? How can you break the cycle of this behavior?

Group Session Model:

This group session was aimed at identifying and recognizing self-defeating behaviors to prevent self-harm. The clinician utilized a process-oriented exercise consisting of handouts with a checklist of self-defeating behaviors to be completed by each member. The group discussion focused on three questions: What do these behaviors say about you? When and why do you use these behaviors? How can you break the cycle of this behavior?

In the session, the patient had his head down and an anguished expression, and at times, he hid his face with his jacket. During the session, he appeared to be tired. The clinician prompted the patient to engage in the group activity and discussion. The patient stated, "I spend excessively on others. I buy things impulsively. I even bought very expensive things, such as cars, trying to buy happiness in my marriage, and nothing worked."

The clinician offered the patient support, empathizing with his disappointment, while helping him to understand the negative impact of his self-defeating behavior in his current life. The patient was able to understand the importance of recognizing and interrupting his self-defeating behaviors to prevent future self-harm.

The future sessions will continue to assist the patient in identifying and recognizing other self-defeating behaviors blocking his stabilization process.

Topic 1: Identifying Inappropriate Behaviors

Exercise 3: Self-Defeating Behaviors

Self-defeating behavior does not mean only hurting your body or doing things to your body that bring you pain. Self-defeating behaviors can also hurt your mind and your social, spiritual, professional, and financial lives. There are many self-defeating behaviors that in a direct or indirect way may harm you. Learning about such self-defeating behaviors can help you to prevent self-harm.

- Complete the tasks below to know more about your self-defeating behaviors.

  ◆ Put a checkmark below next to one of the behaviors that you may have been using.

  ☐ 1. I use alcohol in excess.
  ☐ 2. I smoke to relax.
  ☐ 3. I always procrastinate.
  ☐ 4. I lie to get the things that I need.
  ☐ 5. I talk too much.
  ☐ 6. I have difficulty communicating.
  ☐ 7. I am not organized.
  ☐ 8. I need to have things right away.
  ☐ 9. I refuse to make any changes.
  ☐ 10. I am always seeking attention.
  ☐ 11. I accept everything passively.
  ☐ 12. I use substances to feel better.
  ☐ 13. I do things that may be harmful.
  ☐ 14. I waste time with superficial things.
  ☐ 15. I always try to justify everything.
  ☐ 16. I overeat when I become anxious.
  ☐ 17. I am generally late to my appointments.
  ☐ 18. I overwhelm myself with minor problems.
  ☐ 19. I do not need anybody to help me.
  ☐ 20. I change the subject if is not pleasant.
  ☐ 21. I do not ask for help when I need it.
  ☐ 22. I avoid working toward my goals.
  ☐ 23. I spend too much money.
  ☐ 24. Other _____

  ◆ What do these behaviors say about you?

  ◆ When and why do you use these behaviors?

  ◆ How can you break the cycle of this behavior?

Topic 1: Identifying Inappropriate Behaviors

Exercise 4: Self-Sabotaging Behaviors

Purpose:

    A. To learn ways of self-sabotaging.
    B. To increase knowledge about reasons for self-sabotaging.

Hints and Procedures:

Distribute the handouts provided below, and ask a volunteer from the group to read the information about self-sabotaging behaviors, including the definition. Ask the members to answer this question: how do you know if you are sabotaging? Assist the members in identifying reasons for self-sabotaging (see the reasons in the footnote on the handout).

Group Session Model:

The group session aimed at helping the members to increase awareness of self-sabotaging behaviors. To facilitate the group process, the members were instructed to use handouts with information and questions about self-sabotaging behaviors. The group task consisted of completing a checklist of ways of self-sabotaging followed by a group discussion about reasons for self-sabotaging.

During the session, the patient was neat and clean. At the beginning of the session, he appeared discouraged and distant from the group activity. Upon encouragement by the clinician, the patient became more interested in the topic discussed and was observed being more attentive with spontaneous participation. The patient stated, "My worse self-sabotaging behavior has been to negatively compare myself to others."

The members recognized the patient's self-sabotaging behavior, and the group discussion continued to discuss several other ways of sabotaging as well as possible reasons why people self-sabotage. The patient recognized that learning about this topic helped him understand many of his symptoms, including his lack of motivation, which may have been associated with his self-sabotaging behaviors.

The future sessions will focus on assisting the patient in developing appropriate combined treatments to stop self-sabotaging behaviors and decrease his mental illness symptoms.

Topic 1: Identifying Inappropriate Behaviors

Exercise 4: Self-Sabotaging Behaviors

Are you sabotaging yourself?

Self-sabotaging behaviors are among many of the inappropriate behaviors that can be harmful for oneself. One of the first steps to work on the inappropriate behaviors is to be able to identify them, recognize them, and know their negative consequences.

- Please, answer the questions A–F below:

  A. What is a self-sabotaging behavior?[1]
  B. What are the reasons for self-sabotaging?[2]
  C. When does self-sabotaging behavior occur?[3]
  D. What are the negative consequences of self-sabotaging behaviors?[4]
  E. What sabotaging behaviors below apply to you?

   ☐ 1. Procrastinating on a regular basis.
   ☐ 2. Using excuses for not accepting suggestions.
   ☐ 3. Having a difficult time getting motivated to do the things I really want to do.
   ☐ 4. Seeing myself as different from others for justifying things that would not work for me.
   ☐ 5. Promising myself to succeed, but still not living the life I truly want to live.
   ☐ 6. Just listening to others for the answer that I want to hear.
   ☐ 7. Feeling as if people in my life are constantly criticizing me.
   ☐ 8. Feeling resentful for not having more control over the events in my life.
   ☐ 9. Looking for the negative part of the treatment and ignoring the positive ones.
   ☐ 10. Putting myself in a negative way.

  F. How can you break the cycle of these sabotaging behaviors?

---

[1] The dictionary definition of sabotage is "an act or process tending to hamper or hurt" or "deliberate subversion." Self-sabotaging behavior is irrational.
[2] They may include negative feelings, such as passive anger, fear of failure, accommodation, lack of knowledge, as well as fear of the unknown.
[3] Self-sabotaging behavior occurs when there is no logical or rational explanation for why people cannot do the things they want to do or why they cannot have the things they want to have, or when they refuse to accept these limitations.
[4] They are counterproductive, produce the opposite result, and can decrease your motivation to do the things you really want to do.

Topic 1: Identifying Inappropriate Behaviors

Exercise 5: Argumentative Behaviors

Purpose:

    A. To recognize what can create an argument.
    B. To explore the five steps to avoid an argument.

Hints and Procedures:

While the handouts are being distributed, warm up the group discussion with the techniques of martial arts, and ask the members how to avoid a fight like a martial artist. Assist and encourage the members to complete the steps to avoid an argument with the corresponding behaviors. Promote the group discussion with each step and behaviors to avoid an argument.

Group Session Model:

The subject of this group session was the five steps to avoid an argument. The clinician initiated the group discussion by reviewing with the members the techniques of martial arts to avoid an argument. Then the members were asked to use handouts and complete the five steps with the corresponding behaviors to avoid an argument. The group discussion focused on the content of each step and behavior.

The patient appeared less depressed today. He was alert, attentive, cooperative, and receptive to prompting, and was well oriented to place, person, and thing. In response to the topic, the patient expressed himself by stating, "One way that I try to avoid a possible argument is by staying away from aggressive or strange people."

The members supported the patient's step to avoid an argument. The patient responded positively to praise and agreed to continue working on the five steps to avoid an argument in the future.

Continued psychotherapy is recommended for this patient to monitor his progress, offer him support, improve his behavior, decrease his symptoms, and stabilize his mood.

Topic 1: Identifying Inappropriate Behaviors

Exercise 5: Argumentative Behaviors

To argue or not to argue? That is the question!

How do you avoid an argument? A martial artist fights only when absolutely necessary—when there is no alternative. An argument may start with an argumentative behavior, ending up in a conflict or a fight. The standard defense in karate is to take a step backward or move to the side when someone throws a punch. This step to the side lets the person being attacked think out his or her response. Remember, you may become a victim or a defendant in a lawsuit by fighting. So, do you argue or not argue? And the answer is to avoid it. The steps to avoid an argument below will help you with this matter.

- Please match the behaviors in the first column with the five steps to avoid an argument in the second column.[1]

( ) 1. Be aware of your surroundings.
( ) 2. Stay fit and alert; refrain from alcohol or drug abuse.
( ) 3. Watch people with unusual or inappropriate behaviors.
( ) 4. Tell an attacker in a clear voice that you do not want to argue.
( ) 5. Locate the exits: where is safety in case you need it?
( ) 6. Never provoke or escalate an incident.
( ) 7. Control your actions.
( ) 8. Formulate your escape.
( ) 9. Be aware of angry and aggressive people.
( ) 10. Anticipate what could happen.

a) avoiding risk
b) avoiding provocative behaviors
c) observation of power
d) being cautious
e) ending the conflict

---

[1] Answer key: 1) c, 2) a, 3) d, 4) e, 5) c, 6) b, 7) a, 8) c, 9) b, 10) d.

Topic 1: Identifying Inappropriate Behaviors

Exercise 6: Abusive Behaviors

Purpose:

    A. To identify abusive behaviors in five life dimensions.
    B. To increase awareness of destructive results of abusive behaviors in people's lives.

Hints and Procedures:

Provide the members with the handouts, and use the information from its footnote to promote the group discussion about the abusive behaviors in the following five life dimensions: physical, emotional, sexual, social, and financial. Use the content of each statement to discuss the destructive results of abusive behaviors in a person's life.

Group Session Model:

The group session consisted of a therapeutic approach to healthy maintenance through the discussion of how people utilize abusive behaviors in a controlled manner with destructive results. In order to facilitate the group activity and discussion, the members were asked to use handouts with a list of several abusive behaviors in the following five life dimensions: physical, emotional, sexual, social, and financial. The therapeutic intervention consisted of using debate as a technique to promote the group discussion on the abusive behaviors.

In the session, the patient's mood was depressed. He was observed as initially guarded, reclusive, and focusing on his own thoughts. As the session progressed and upon encouragement by his peers, he became engaged in the process of reviewing the abusive behaviors from the handouts. The patient made the following comment: "Cheating on your partner is an abusive sexual behavior."

The members discussed the patient's comment and other forms of abusive behaviors leading to negative consequences in a person's life. The patient concurred with the other members' forms of abusive behaviors discussed.

The staff will continue to assist the patient with therapeutic interventions aimed at replacing his inappropriate behaviors with behaviors that can lead to mood stabilization.

Topic 1: Identifying Inappropriate Behaviors

Exercise 6: Abusive Behaviors

The Five Dimensions of Abusive Behaviors

What is an abusive behavior? An abusive behavior is not a symptom; it is a choice to exert power and control over someone. There are many kinds of abusive behaviors that have destructive results in a person's life. They may include the physical, emotional, sexual, social, and financial.[1] You might review the list below in order to know more about these abusive and destructive behaviors.

- Please use the letters A, B, C, D, and E below from the second column related to the five life dimensions to match the abusive behaviors in the first column.[2]

(　) 1. Monitoring the victim's mail or phone calls	A = Physical
(　) 2. Monitoring the victim's spending	B = Emotional
(　) 3. Pushing, restraining, punching, and slapping	C = Sexual
(　) 4. Making jokes about the victim	D = Social
(　) 5. Insulting the victim	E = Financial
(　) 6. Shaking, sustained beating, and kicking the victim	
(　) 7. Criticizing the victim's sexuality	
(　) 8. Ignoring the victim's feelings	
(　) 9. Treating the partner as a sex object	
(　) 10. Forbidding the victim to see friends and family	
(　) 11. Controlling the victim's access to cash	
(　) 12. Spying on the victim or his or her friends	
(　) 13. Demanding sex	
(　) 14. Lying about finances	

✧ What can be the destructive results of the above behaviors in a person's life?

---

[1] The physical abuse often begins with less violent assaults, such as pushing. As the abuse continues, it becomes increasingly violent. The emotional abuse is a tool used by those who want to make their partners feel scared, worthless, and crazy. The abuser's goal is to control the victim. The sexual abuse is one of the least discussed but most common forms of abusive behavior. The social abuse is used to isolate the victim from others in the community. Financial abusers often attempt to establish financial control over the victims. The victims who are financially dependent on the abusers have fewer resources for escape.

[2] Answer key: 1) D, 2) B, 3) A, 4) B, 5) B, 6) A, 7) C, 8) B, 9) C, 10) D, 11) E, 12) D, 13) C, 14) E.

Topic 1: Identifying Inappropriate Behaviors

Exercise 7: Defensive Behaviors

Purpose:

    A. To discuss components of defensive behaviors.
    B. To decrease defensive behaviors by identifying justifications.

Hints and Procedures:

Warm up the group discussion with a definition of "defensiveness." Distribute the handouts provided below, and promote the group discussion with the content of each question related to defensive behaviors. Ask the members if they have been using any defensive behavior and why.

Group Session Model:

The group session focused on decreasing defensive behaviors by identifying justifications. The members were provided with handouts with information and questions related to defensive behaviors and justifications for using them. They were asked if they have been using any defensive behaviors and why. The group discussion focused on the content of each question.

The patient was appropriately groomed and well dressed, had direct eye contact, and was well oriented to person, time, and place. However, the patient had a low energy level and a moderate level of depression as evidenced by his sad affect. The patient focused on his low level of self-confidence as a justification for using defensive behavior. The patient admitted, "I think I have been using defensive behaviors as a result of my lack of self-confidence." The patient continued his idea by saying, "Sometimes I have feelings of inadequacy simply because I am not as young as I used to be."

The therapeutic intervention consisted of reviewing mechanisms of adjustment, venting of thoughts and feelings, and support to decrease the use of defensive behaviors, to which the patient was receptive.

Continued psychotherapy sessions are recommended for this patient in order to decrease his defensive behaviors, decrease his mental illness symptoms, monitor his progress, and reach his mood stabilization.

Topic 1: Identifying Inappropriate Behaviors

Exercise 7: Defensive Behaviors

Defensiveness is often a reflection of insecurity in individuals. It tends to distort questions into accusations and responses into justifications.

- Answer the questions below to learn more about the defensive behaviors.

    1. Why are people defensive?
    2. What can be the result of defensive behaviors?
    3. Can defensiveness be justified, and if so, in which circumstances?
    4. What can be the sources of defensive behaviors?
    5. Can fear of a loss of status lead to defensive behaviors? How?
    6. Can fear of rejection lead to defensive behaviors? Why?
    7. Can lack of self-confidence lead to defensive behaviors? How?
    8. Can the need to prove or impress others lead to defensive behaviors? Why?
    9. Can perfectionism lead to defensive behaviors? How?
    10. How can we cope with defensive behaviors?

Topic 1: Identifying Inappropriate Behaviors

Exercise 8: Decompensating Behaviors

Purpose:

    A. To increase awareness of behaviors impairing a daily level of functioning.
    B. To identify behaviors that can directly or indirectly lead to decompensation.

Hints and Procedures:

Warm up the group discussion by asking the members this question: "How are you functioning?" Distribute the handouts provided below, and briefly discuss the concept of "decompensation" (e.g., gradual process, impaired functioning). Ask the members to identify their own behaviors indicating an impaired daily level of functioning and why they think such behaviors can lead to decompensation.

Group Session Model:

The group session was aimed at assisting the members in increasing awareness of behaviors impairing their daily levels of functioning. The clinician warmed up the group discussion by asking the members this question: "How are you functioning?" The members were given handouts with a list of behaviors that can directly or indirectly lead to decompensation. The group discussion focused on finding out why such behaviors could lead to decompensation.

In the session, the patient was observed as guarded, somewhat suspicious, and distracted. He reported poor sleep last night, had a sad facial expression, and was agitated. The clinician encouraged the patient to identify at least one behavior indicating impaired functioning. The patient expressed himself by stating, "Well, I am schizophrenic and sometimes, I become paranoid and that has impaired my ability to function." The patient continued his idea by saying, "Not too long ago, I had to be hospitalized because of my intensive paranoia."

The members concurred with the patient's opinion. The patient was receptive to the support received. Also, he agreed to take responsibility to work on improving his impaired level of functioning.

Currently, the patient continues to demonstrate impaired functioning; thus, continued psychotherapy sessions are recommended for this patient to prevent decompensation of his mental illness symptoms.

Topic 1: Identifying Inappropriate Behaviors

Exercise 8: Decompensating Behaviors

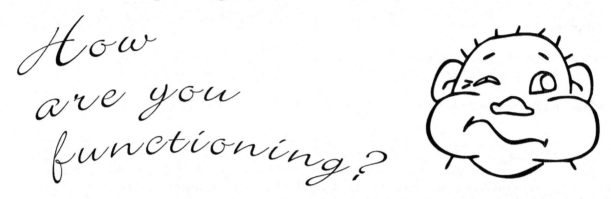

Identifying behaviors indicating a decrease in your daily level of functioning will help you to prevent decompensation or further exacerbation of mental illness symptoms or psychiatric hospitalization. There are many behaviors that can directly, indirectly, or gradually lead to decompensation.

- **Please answer the three following questions:**

  ⬥ Can you identify at least two behaviors below that can lead to decompensation?

1. Being apprehensive	10. Being restless	18. Being suspicious
2. Being paranoid	11. Being agitated	19. Being passive
3. Being isolated	12. Being withdrawn	20. Being irritable
4. Being dependent	13. Being aggressive	21. Being impatient
5. Being resistant	14. Being defensive	22. Being impulsive
6. Being intolerant	15. Being inconsistent	23. Denying
7. Procrastinating	16. Minimizing	24. Ignoring
8. Not sleeping well	17. Not eating well	25. Other _____
9. Not concentrating well		

  ⬥ Why do you think these behaviors can lead to decompensation?

  ⬥ How can you work on these behaviors?

Topic 2: Working on Inappropriate Behaviors

Exercise 1: Behaviors and the Treatment

Purpose:

    A. To discuss and modify inappropriate behaviors interfering with the treatment process.

Hints and Procedures:

    Distribute the handouts provided below. Ask the members to identify behaviors that directly or indirectly may have been interfering with the success of their treatment. Promote the group discussion on how to modify or decrease inappropriate behaviors by using specific strategies (see footnote from handout).

Group Session Model:

    The group session consisted of discussing and modifying the members' inappropriate behaviors interfering with their treatment process. The clinician introduced the topic by reviewing with the members how many inappropriate behaviors can have a direct or indirect negative influence on their treatment process and lives. Examples of negative influences were provided. The group discussion focused on exploring strategies to modify the inappropriate behaviors.

    In prior sessions, the patient came in depressed. Similarly, in this session, the patient was observed with a flat affect, was sitting erect with fair eye contact and a sad facial expression, and was initially isolated. On approach, the patient stated, "I think I have been procrastinating too much. Because of my depression, I always postpone important things to do and end up getting nothing accomplished."

    The clinician assisted the patient with cognitive behavioral interventions aimed at promoting positive thoughts to modify his inappropriate behaviors. The patient was receptive to these interventions and stated that he was going to continue practicing the strategies discussed during the group session.

    The professional team will continue to assist the patient with therapeutic interventions aimed at modifying inappropriate behaviors interfering with the patient's treatment progress.

Topic 2: Working on Inappropriate Behaviors

Exercise 1: Behaviors and the Treatment

My Behaviors and my Treatment

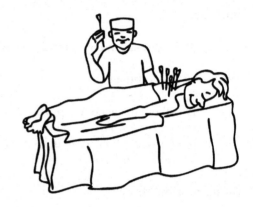

The success of your treatment will depend on your ability to identify, modify, or decrease inappropriate behaviors. There are many behaviors that in a direct or indirect way can interfere with your treatment process. What are they, and how can you modify or decrease them? Let's try to work on these behaviors today.

- Please complete the statements below:

  ◆ Some of the negative behaviors interfering with my treatment are

    1. Isolation
    2. Procrastination
    3. Impulsiveness
    4. Aggressiveness
    5. Lack of discipline
    6. Withdrawal
    7. Non-compliance with my treatment
    8. Non-compliance with my medication
    9. Lack of implementing goals
    10. Lack of commitment
    11. Lack of consistency
    12. Other _____

  ◆ I can use the following strategies to decrease these inappropriate behaviors:[1]

    For behavior number ( ), I can _____
    For behavior number ( ), I can _____
    For behavior number ( ), I can _____

---

[1] Some strategies to decrease inappropriate behaviors may include internalization of positive messages; education, such as acquisition of knowledge and new information; changes of attitude, perceptions, values, and thoughts; relaxation techniques; development of disciplines and goals.

Topic 2: Working on Inappropriate Behaviors

Exercise 2: Changing Behaviors

Purpose:

    A. To discuss concepts of change.
    B. To develop measures to change inappropriate behaviors.

Hints and Procedures:

While the handouts are being distributed, warm up the group discussion with concepts of change—i.e., can people change? Challenge each member to identify at least one inappropriate behavior he or she wants to change. Assist the members in identifying measures to change the inappropriate behaviors (see footnote from handout for possible measures).

Group Session Model:

This group session was aimed at assisting the members in developing measures to change inappropriate behaviors. The members were provided with handouts containing information and questions about changing inappropriate behaviors. The clinician introduced the topic by reviewing the foundation of changes related to inappropriate behaviors, such as the question of whether people can change behaviors. Each member was asked to identify at least one behavior and measures to make the change effective.

The patient came to the session with fleeting eyes and sitting uptight. He was sad and isolated from the members. However, the patient was able to identify one of his defeating behaviors and understand the use of the measure "letting go of the behavior" to change it. Upon approach, the patient commented, "Now, I am convinced that I need let go of the need for retaliation against my wife because of her betrayal of me."

The members empathized with the patient's feelings and concerns. The patient was receptive to the group support. Also, he agreed to begin using other measures discussed during the group discussion to change his defeating behaviors.

Based on the staff observation, the patient continues to demonstrate impaired coping methods and a poor level of functioning, so this level of intervention will be required to improve his ability to function and prevent a psychiatric hospitalization.

120 ■ *Group Behavior*

Topic 2: Working on Inappropriate Behaviors

Exercise 2: Changing Behaviors

How can we change inappropriate behaviors?

The process of changing behaviors may be gradual, requiring time, commitment, and patience. Changing inappropriate behaviors may also require multiple measures, increased knowledge, and the willingness to make any realistic change.

- By the way ...

    1. Can people change behaviors? Why?
    2. How can people change behaviors?
    3. Why do some people never change their behaviors?
    4. Should we try to change people's behaviors? Explain.
    5. What should be the first practical step to make a real change in behavior?
    6. What behavior do you first want to change? Why?
    7. What are the benefits of changing this behavior?
    8. Can you identify at least two measures to change this behavior?[1]

---

[1] They may include letting go of the behavior, assertiveness, avoidance, time out, relaxation activities, positive self-talking, thought stopping, thought replacement, and using less internal focus.

Topic 2: Working on Inappropriate Behaviors

Exercise 3: Coping Behaviors

Purpose:

    A. To use coping behaviors to decrease inappropriate behaviors.
    B. To control inappropriate behaviors.

Hints and Procedures:

Provide the members with the handouts. Challenge the members to identify inappropriate behaviors that may apply to them. Encourage each member to practice at least one coping behavior during the group session. Review the benefits of the exercise.

Group Session Model:

The subject of this group session was coping behaviors. The members were provided with handouts with a guide and an exercise to practice the use of coping behaviors to eliminate or decrease inappropriate behaviors. Each member was encouraged to practice the exercise during the session.

The patient spoke in a hesitant manner, fidgeted constantly, and had a predominantly anxious mood. In response to the topic discussed, the patient commented on one inappropriate behavior and a coping behavior as follows: "I think I talk too much, and sometimes, I just respond very fast. Life has taught me to remain calm. I am trying to practice appropriate listening skills by listening to other people to get a better understanding of what they want to tell me."

Positive social reinforcement was provided by the members regarding the patient's use of appropriate listening skills as a coping behavior to cope with excessive talking. The patient was receptive to the reinforcement and recognized the need to continue practicing the use of coping behaviors to decrease other inappropriate behaviors.

The future sessions will continue to provide the patient with therapeutic approaches aimed at reducing the patient's inappropriate behaviors as part of his stabilization process.

Topic 2: Working on Inappropriate Behaviors

Exercise 3: Coping Behaviors

The use of coping behaviors can help avoid the escalation of inappropriate behaviors. The exercise that follows is an opportunity to record your best and most successful coping behaviors that can be used to prevent or decrease inappropriate behaviors.

- **Please complete tasks A and B:**

    A. Identify one inappropriate behavior below:

a) Aggressiveness	e) Impulsiveness	i) Restlessness
b) Rudeness	f) Impatience	j) Unassertiveness
c) Disrespect	g) Intolerance	k) Excessive talking
d) Procrastination	h) Isolation	l) Other _____

    B. Use the inappropriate behavior you have identified above and fill in the space provided with the coping behaviors below:

    ◆ In order to cope with _____ I can

    1. use an appropriate voice by _____
    2. use an appropriate language by _____
    3. use appropriate listening skills by _____
    4. avoid the escalation of a situation by _____
    5. express my needs by _____
    6. suggest a solution or a compromise by _____
    7. try to express an understanding by _____
    8. describe a problem without blaming others by _____
    9. make a compromise by _____
    10. other _____

- **Continue using the coping behaviors above to cope with other inappropriate behaviors that may apply to you.**

Topic 3: Learning New and Positive Behaviors

Exercise 1: Effective Disciplining

Purpose:

    A. To develop self-discipline.
    B. To discuss concepts, steps, and rules for effective self-disciplining.

Hints and Procedures:

Distribute the handouts provided below, and read the text related to effective self-disciplining. Promote the group discussion by using the questions related to concepts, steps, and rules for effective self-disciplining. Challenge the members to apply the concepts, steps, and rules for effective self-disciplining. In this manner, they can learn new and positive behaviors in their lives. For instance, they can learn how to be assertive, how to make new friends, and how to increase their social support system.

Group Session Model:

This group session consisted of developing effective self-discipline. The clinician warmed up the group discussion by reviewing important information related to the use of discipline in life. The members were given handouts with information and questions related to effective self-discipline. The members were challenged to identify and incorporate new and positive behaviors in their lives by applying the concepts, steps, and rules discussed.

Although the patient was alert and attentive, he showed a moderate depressed mood as evidenced by a sad facial expression and rigid posture, and he was initially isolated. The patient was attentive, receptive, and responsive to the group discussion with minimum prompting. The patient stated, "I have been very isolated because of my depression, but now, it is time to learn how to make new friends, and I learned that I need to be committed to do what I need to do if I want to succeed in life."

The members concurred with the patient's concept of "commitment" as a valuable step to develop effective self-discipline. The patient was receptive to the support received.

Continued group psychotherapy sessions are recommended for this patient to monitor his progress, and offer him support and reinforcement to learn new and positive behaviors in order to decrease his mental illness symptoms.

Topic 3: Learning New and Positive Behaviors

Exercise 1: Effective Disciplining

The Steps and the Rules for Disciplining

Success in life, as well as the ability to learn new behaviors and become stable, depends directly on the use of effective concepts, steps, and rules to discipline oneself. They may include self-control, understanding, commitment, consistency, persistence, and enforcement. Are you familiar with these?

- Please, let's try to answer the following questions:

    1. What does "effective disciplining" mean?
    2. What are the benefits of using effective discipline?
    3. How can we use self-control for effective discipline?
    4. How can we make rules for effective discipline?
    5. How can we make sure that we understand the rules?
    6. How can we be committed?
    7. How can we say no to ourselves when we are thinking of breaking the rules?
    8. How can we continue if we are failing? Or, how can we be persistent?
    9. How can we be ready to enforce the rules?
    10. Where should we start again if we fail?

Topic 3: Learning New and Positive Behaviors

Exercise 2: Learning to Be Responsible for Behaviors

Purpose:

    A. To assume responsibility for personal behaviors.

Hints and Procedures:

Warm up the group discussion by reviewing concepts of realistic versus unrealistic, workable versus unworkable, and appropriate versus inappropriate behaviors. Use the handouts provided below to facilitate the group discussion. Encourage the members to identify behaviors that they should be responsible for as part of their treatment process, as well as to come up with alternative ways to assume responsibilities for such behaviors.

Group Session Model:

The focus of this group session was on encouraging the members to assume responsibility for their personal behaviors as part of their treatment process. In order to facilitate the group tasks and discussion, the members were given handouts with a list of workable and unworkable behaviors and were asked to identify the ones they should be responsible for. Also, during the group discussion, the members were encouraged to come up with alternative ways to assume responsibilities for the appropriate and workable behaviors discussed.

In the session, the patient had a moderate level of depression. He displayed an attentive facial expression but a low-key demeanor. He was observed having tight lips, sitting erect, and staring at the clinician and his peers. On approach, the patient stated, "I have been trying to learn effective coping skills to better cope with my symptoms, and I understand that this is my responsibility." Also, the patient described how he has been trying to learn effective coping skills by being attentive to the group discussions.

Reassurance, encouragement, positive feedback, and support were among the therapeutic interventions utilized. The patient was receptive to the intervention as he was able to remain attentive to the group discussion.

The professional team will continue to assist the patient with therapeutic interventions aimed at engaging him in group discussion as part of his treatment process.

Topic 3: Learning New and Positive Behaviors

Exercise 2: Learning to Be Responsible for Behaviors

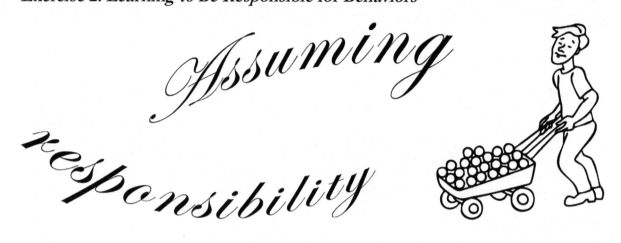

The success of your treatment will depend on you to assume responsibility for certain effective and realistic behaviors. What behaviors should you be responsible for?

- Analyze the means of behaviors from the list below.

    ◆ Means of behaviors:

    1. Changing myself
    2. Changing other people's lives
    3. Listening to what others are trying to say
    4. Attending this group psychotherapy session once in awhile
    5. Self-disclosing in the group process
    6. Being quiet and not talking
    7. Complying with my medication
    8. Waiting for a miracle
    9. Learning effective coping skills
    10. Implementing goals only after being discharged

    ◆ Now, answer the following questions:

    A. Which means of behaviors are effective? Why?
    B. Which means of behaviors are less effective or should be avoided? Why?
    C. Which means of behaviors should you be responsible for? Why?
    D. How can you assume responsibility for the effective means of behaviors?

Topic 3: Learning New and Positive Behaviors

Exercise 3: Appropriate Behaviors

Purpose:

    A. To discuss appropriate behaviors among group members.
    B. To learn and practice new and appropriate behaviors.

Hints and Procedures:

Start the group discussion by asking the members to identify some benefits of learning new and appropriate behaviors. Provide the members with the handouts, and encourage them to identify any new and appropriate behaviors they have been learning or practicing.

Group Session Model:

The group session was developed in order to discuss appropriate behaviors among group members. The clinician started the group discussion by reviewing some benefits of learning new and appropriate behaviors. To facilitate the group activities and processes, the members were provided with handouts containing a list of several appropriate behaviors. They were encouraged to select and share with each other any new and appropriate behaviors they have been implementing.

The patient's affect was sad, and his mood was depressed, more so than in previous group sessions. The patient was fatigued and lethargic, indicating a low energy level. The patient required some encouragement to engage in the group discussion. The patient stated, "I have been practicing assertiveness to overcome problems in my social relationships."

Although the patient demonstrated a low level of energy during the group session, he asked relevant questions and was able to develop a positive attitude to increase his assertive behaviors.

The future group sessions will continue to assist the patient in learning new and appropriate behaviors in order to improve his level of functioning.

Topic 3: Learning New and Positive Behaviors

Exercise 3: Appropriate Behaviors

Appropriate behaviors are always welcome in any level of our society. They are pleasant and can bring us many benefits. Learning new and appropriate behaviors should be an endless process in our lives. What is your opinion about that?

- Have you been able to learn any new and appropriate behaviors here in this group?

    I have been practicing the following behaviors:

    ☐ 1. Being assertive   ☐ 8. Giving suggestions   ☐ 15. Being attentive
    ☐ 2. Being punctual   ☐ 9. Being kind   ☐ 16. Giving positive feedback
    ☐ 3. Being supportive   ☐ 10. Being consistent   ☐ 17. Being persistent
    ☐ 4. Being committed   ☐ 11. Being receptive   ☐ 18. Developing discipline
    ☐ 5. Complimenting   ☐ 12. Listening to others   ☐ 19. Respecting others
    ☐ 6. Being tolerant   ☐ 13. Interacting   ☐ 20. Being friendly
    ☐ 7. Praising   ☐ 14. Cooperating   ☐ Other _____

    ✧ Wow! You have been doing so well!

    ✧ How have you been implementing these behaviors?

        Behavior (   ): I have been _____
        Behavior (   ): I have been _____
        Behavior (   ): I have been _____

Topic 3: Learning New and Positive Behaviors

Exercise 4: Cooperative Behaviors

Purpose:

    A. To learn how to develop cooperation.
    B. To discuss cooperation among group members.
    C. To identify the benefits of being cooperative.

Hints and Procedures:

Promote the initial group discussion with the following statement: "We are social human beings by nature. It is practically impossible to live in this world without depending on other people." Distribute the handouts provided below, and continue the group discussion by using the questions related to cooperative behaviors. Discuss the benefits of being cooperative (see handout footnote).

Group Session Model:

The group session was focused on helping the members develop cooperation by using the cooperative behaviors exercise. The members were encouraged to use handouts, answer questions, and share ideas on several concepts related to being cooperative, including the benefits and how to develop cooperative behaviors.

For this session, the patient was initially sitting apart from his peers with a tense posture and a sad affect. As the session progressed, the patient appeared interested in the topic being discussed and had moderate participation. His comments, although brief, were appropriate. He stated, "For me, close cooperation means really paying attention when people talk here, and as a result, I am learning more about my mental problem."

Others in the group stated additional benefits gained from close cooperation with others, including saving time and having an enjoyable moment. The patient was receptive to the concepts and new information obtained.

The staff has determined that the patient will need to continue to be assisted with further therapeutic interventions in an effort to promote the learning of new appropriate behaviors to decrease his mental illness symptoms and reach his mood stabilization.

Topic 3: Learning New and Positive Behaviors

Exercise 4: Cooperative Behaviors

We live in a society in which in a direct or indirect way, we all depend on each other to live. It is practically impossible to live in this world without depending on other people. We depend on our families, friends, professionals, authorities, government, and so on. Therefore, it is important to learn how to be cooperative. Don't you think so?

- **Developing Cooperation**

    1. What does it mean to be cooperative?
    2. Again, why should we be cooperative?
    3. What can we gain by working cooperatively?[1]
    4. How can we develop cooperation at home?
    5. How can we develop cooperation at work?
    6. How can we develop cooperation at a recreational setting?
    7. How can we develop cooperation here in this group?
    8. What happens when someone is uncooperative in this group? What should we do?
    9. What else do you know about cooperative behaviors?
    10. Are you cooperative? Why do you think so?

---

[1] We can save time, think of more alternatives to a specific problem, have good time, and know people better.

Topic 3: Learning New and Positive Behaviors

Exercise 5: Alternative Behaviors

Purpose:

A. To discuss alternative behaviors to cope with mental illness symptoms.

Hints and Procedures:

Warm up the group discussion with this statement: "I would rather be fishing than crying! How about you?" Distribute the handouts provided below. Ask the members to identify some of their symptoms and apply the behaviors from the list to cope with them. Assist each member by providing information on how to implement each behavior being discussed.

Group Session Model:

The group session's objective was aimed at discussing alternative behaviors to cope with mental illness symptoms. The clinician warmed up the group discussion with a phrase that made the concept of alternative behaviors easy to understand: "I would rather be fishing than crying." Then the members were provided with handouts with a list of several behaviors to cope with mental illness symptoms. The members were asked to identify some of their symptoms and apply the behaviors from the list to cope with them. Also, the clinician assisted each member by providing information on how to implement the behaviors discussed.

The patient had a disheveled appearance and a depressed mood and affect. The patient required reassurance and some guidance in order to participate in the group activity. The patient stated, "One of my symptoms is isolation. I think I need to make new friends to help me with that."

The discussion focused on how and where to make new friends, such as inside the group and extending to other settings in the community. The patient was receptive to the suggestions received and agreed to explore them in the future.

The staff will continue to work with the patient to increase the use of alternative behaviors in order to reduce his mental illness symptoms, so that his daily functional level improves.

Topic 3: Learning New and Positive Behaviors

Exercise 5: Alternative Behaviors

I would rather be fishing than crying! How about you?

You can use many alternative behaviors to cope with your mental illness symptoms. Many behaviors can be fun and very enjoyable. They may include some of your hobbies and activities of your interest. Increasing knowledge about such alternative behaviors will help you with your stabilization process.

- Please complete the following statements:

    ✧ One of my symptoms is _____

    ✧ I can use two behaviors below to cope with this symptom.

1. Fishing	9. Praying	17. Sharing and talking
2. Watching TV	10. Meditating	18. Attending AA/NA meetings
3. Walking	11. Visiting friends	19. Spending time with family
4. Reading	12. Playing with kids	20. Making new friends
5. Running	13. Listening to music	21. Going out (to where?)
6. Swimming	14. Attending church	22. Doing activities to relax
7. Socializing	15. Eating healthy	23. Getting active (in what?)
8. Bicycling	16. Jogging	24. Other _____

    ✧ How can you implement these two behaviors?

Topic 3: Learning New and Positive Behaviors

Exercise 6: Positive Role Models

Purpose:

    A. To use positive role models to learn new and positive behaviors.

Hints and Procedures:

While the handouts are being passed out, start the group discussion with two statements: "We are true imitators!" and "We learn from other people!" Assist and encourage the members to think about outstanding personages in the community that they admire. Encourage each member to identify at least three positive behaviors from each personage and discuss strategies to implement them.

Group Session Model:

The group session's activity consisted of encouraging the members to use role models to learn new and positive behaviors. In order to facilitate the group activity, the members were asked to think about outstanding personages in the community that they admire. Each member was encouraged to identify three positive behaviors from each personage that they would like to imitate and how to implement the behaviors.

The patient was observed as being alert, calm, and quiet, and having a sad facial expression, but he was responsive and able to offer occasional feedback to other members. The patient stated, "Currently, my positive role model has been my psychotherapist from whom I would like to learn more about how to be independent, stable, and disciplined."

The clinician assisted the patient by discussing some valuable strategies to implement the behaviors discussed. Improving coping skills, gaining knowledge, and developing goals were some of the strategies discussed. The patient was receptive to the therapeutic intervention.

Based on the patient's current depressive mental status, the professional team has recommended that the patient continue with this level of service to decrease his mental illness symptoms and prevent exacerbation of them.

Topic 3: Learning New and Positive Behaviors

Exercise 6: Positive Role Models

Using positive role models can be an effective way of learning new and positive behaviors.

A positive role model can provide us with values, concepts, and guidance in developing meaningful positive behaviors and personal standards in life.

- Think about an outstanding personage in the community that you admire. Try to describe three positive behaviors from that person that you would like to imitate or implement in your life. But, please be realistic!

    ⬥ The person that I admire a lot in our community is
    _____

    ⬥ The positive behaviors that I would like to implement are
    Behavior 1: _____
    Behavior 2: _____
    Behavior 3: _____

    ⬥ Some strategies that I can use to implement these behaviors are
    Strategy 1: _____
    Strategy 2: _____
    Strategy 3: _____

Topic 3: Learning New and Positive Behaviors

Exercise 7: Daily Care Needs

Purpose:

    A. To learn and implement behaviors for daily care needs.

Hints and Procedures:

    Distribute the handouts provided below. Use the questions and review with the members the basic behaviors for an adult's daily living needs (see footnote from handout). Increase the members' motivation by focusing on the excitement and joyful experience of living an independent life. Encourage the members to answer the questions as a guide to learn and implement behaviors for their daily care needs.

Group Session Model:

    The group session focused on the importance of learning and implementing behaviors for daily care needs. At the beginning of the session, the members were asked to review some basic behaviors for an adult's daily living needs followed by a brief discussion about the excitement and joyful experience of living an independent life. Then the members were encouraged to use handouts and answer questions as a guide to learn and implement behaviors for daily care needs.

    The patient appeared sad and quiet, had downcast eyes and slow psychomotor movements, and was isolated. Also, his depressed mood had been apparent in prior sessions. In response to this group session activity, the patient stated, "I used to live alone before. So, I have been able to learn many things to survive, but like everybody else, I still need to learn many other behaviors for my daily care needs since I have been living in an adult living facility for a long time."

    During the course of the group activity, the patient demonstrated a reasonable knowledge of many behaviors for daily care needs by answering the questions from the handout. The clinician offered the patient support, provided feedback, and urged the patient to utilize the group process as a tool to gain support and motivation to implement the behaviors discussed. The patient nodded in acknowledgement of this suggestion.

    The future sessions will continue to focus on helping and encouraging the patient to identify and implement effective behaviors for his daily care needs.

Topic 3: Learning New and Positive Behaviors

Exercise 7: Daily Care Needs

MY GUIDE FOR MY DAILY CARE NEEDS

Are you intending to live by yourself? Living alone can be an exciting and enjoyable experience in life if you know the behaviors for your daily care needs. The guide below will help you learn the behaviors for your daily care needs.

- **Try to answer the following questions:**

    1. Can you describe at least five activities of daily living?[1]
    2. Which ones do you need to learn, and how can you learn them?
    3. Do you know how to cook? How are you going to get your daily meals?
    4. How are you going to maintain yourself financially?
    5. How are you going to pay your bills?
    6. What is your plan for recreational activities?
    7. What do you plan to do on weekends?
    8. How are you going to comply with your treatment?
    9. How are you going to go out for shopping or appointments?
    10. What is your plan for crisis intervention (suicidal ideas, cravings)?

---

[1] They may include daily showering, shaving, cooking, cleaning, dressing, grooming, etc.

Topic 4: Discussing Progress of Using New Behaviors

Exercise 1: Supportive Behaviors

Purpose:

    A. To discuss behaviors that supports a sense of well-being.
    B. To develop behaviors to increase a sense of well-being.

Hints and Procedures:

Provide the members with the handouts. Initiate the group discussion about how the development of supportive behaviors can increase positive feelings and the sense of well-being. Use the list of positive feelings to train the members in developing behaviors to improve those feelings and the sense of well-being.

Group Session Model:

The group session was aimed at helping the members to identify and discuss behaviors that support a sense of well-being. In order to facilitate the group discussion, the members were asked to use handouts containing a list of several positive feelings. The members were encouraged to develop supportive behaviors to improve those positive feelings and the sense of well-being.

During the session, the patient presented to the group with a dominant depressed mood, which can be described as an initially quiet behavior, sad facial expression, and rigid posture. However, the patient was cooperative when prompted and affable when he was speaking. The patient stated, "Well, I believe that socializing is one of the behaviors that can lead to a sense of belonging and increase a sense of well-being."

The patient's opinion was supported and reinforced by the members. The patient was receptive to the feedback received. Also, he was supportive to other members by concurring with them with several other supportive behaviors discussed, such as working on personal projects, participating in activities, and making new friends.

The future sessions will continue to provide the patient with new opportunities to learn new behaviors that support a sense of well-being.

Topic 4: Discussing Progress of Using New Behaviors

Exercise 1: Supportive Behaviors

My Well-Beings Supportive Behaviors

Supportive behaviors can lead to several positive feelings, including the feeling of well-being. But, what supportive behaviors should we implement to develop the feeling of well-being? First, we need to identify some of the positive feelings that contribute to the feeling of well-being. Then we need to implement the supportive behaviors in order to develop these feelings. How can we do that?

- In the list below, there are some of the feelings that contribute to the feeling of well-being. It is very good that all we need to do is to implement behaviors to develop such feelings. The first one is already done. Now, it is your turn.

    ◇ What supportive behaviors should we implement to develop the feeling of

    1. self-belonging? *Becoming involved in a group of activities.*
    2. self-satisfaction? _____
    3. self-accomplishment? _____
    4. self-improvement? _____
    5. self-confidence? _____
    6. self-determination? _____
    7. self-fulfillment? _____
    8. self-recognition? _____
    9. self-pride? _____
    10. self-worth? _____

Topic 4: Discussing Progress of Using New Behaviors

Exercise 2: Learning Is an Endless Process

Purpose:

    A. To discuss learning as an endless process.
    B. To reinforce the acquisition of new and positive behaviors.

Hints and Procedures:

While the handouts are being passed out, warm up the group discussion with the concept "learning is an endless process." Encourage the members to share any new and positive behaviors they have been learning. Review the benefits of learning these new behaviors.

Group Session Model:

This group session's purpose was to reinforce the acquisition of new and positive behaviors among the members. Handouts with information and questions about the learning process were distributed. The clinician warmed up the group discussion with the concept "learning is an endless process in life." The members were encouraged to share any new positive behaviors they have been learning and process the benefits of using the new behaviors.

The patient appeared initially isolated with a sad affect. During the course of the group activity, the patient spoke in an unsure manner. He was observed as being agitated and talking very loudly. The patient identified one new positive behavior that he has learned during his participation in the group process. The patient commented, "Here, I learned how to listen to others, which has helped me learn more about my mental illness and how to better cope with my symptoms."

The patient received support from his peers concerning his new behavior. The patient was receptive to the support.

The professional team will continue to assist the patient in the implementation of other positive behaviors discussed as part of the learning process to improve his functional level and reach mood stabilization.

Topic 4: Discussing Progress of Using New Behaviors

Exercise 2: Learning Is an Endless Process

Learning new and positive behaviors is an endless process in life. This group behavior session and other groups offer a great opportunity to learn new and positive behaviors. Sharing with your peers your new learned behaviors will provide you with motivation to continue learning and improving yourself.

- Let's talk about learning.

- Please, select at least one question to discuss with your peers.

    1. Why is it important to learn?
    2. How do people learn?
    3. What can impede people from learning?
    4. How can we motivate people to learn?
    5. What behaviors can people learn in this group?
    6. Have you learned any new and positive behaviors here? If not, why?
    7. What have been the benefits of learning these new behaviors?
    8. How have these behaviors helped you with your stabilization process?
    9. What behaviors do you still want to learn here? Why?
    10. What is one of your suggestions to learn new behaviors here?

PART VI

GROUP GOALS

TOPICS 1–4

WITH

SIXTEEN EXERCISES

Topic 1: Learning Principles to Goal Setting

Exercise 1: Concepts of Goals

Purpose:

    A. To discuss concepts of goal setting.
    B. To use goal setting to improve daily functioning.

Hints and Procedures:

Use the handouts provided below to facilitate the group discussion on concepts related to goal setting. Discuss concepts including the principles and benefits of goal setting. Ask each member to recall a shot-term or long-term personal goal and apply the concepts discussed.

Group Session Model:

The group session was aimed at discussing concepts of goal setting. The clinician provided the members with handouts containing several questions on the concepts of goals. The members were encouraged to discuss concepts including the principles and benefits of goal setting.

The patient's mood and affect were depressed, and he was consistent with his sad facial expression, and nonspontaneous and timid behaviors. Also, his motivation seemed low. The patient was receptive to moderate prompting and came up with one benefit to goal setting by stating, "I believe goals can help us increase self-esteem."

The patient's opinion was supported by the members. Also, the patient recognized many other benefits of goal setting discussed by the members, including the following: goals can give purpose and direction in life, improve daily functioning, and help stabilize mood.

The professional team will continue to encourage the patient to implement effective goals as part of the process to help him stabilize his mood and affect.

Topic 1: Learning Principles to Goal Setting

Exercise 1: Concepts of Goals

The success of your treatment will depend on your knowledge about goal setting and goal development.

- Try to answer the questions below concerning important concepts related to goals.

    1. What are the benefits of goal development?
    2. What may impede people in the development of goals?
    3. Why is it helpful to set daily goals?
    4. How can we use the concept of "time" in setting goals?
    5. How can we use the concept of "quantity" in setting goals?
    6. How can we use the concept of "frequency" in setting goals?
    7. How can we use the concept of "step by step" in setting goals?
    8. How can we increase motivation to develop goals?
    9. How can we set priorities?
    10. How can we be committed to implement goals?
    11. How can we be consistent in implementing goals?
    12. How can we be persistent in implementing goals?
    13. What is meant by good planning? How can this pay off?
    14. When should people change their goals?
    15. When should people try harder to achieve their goals?

Topic 1: Learning Principles to Goal Setting

Exercise 2: Steps to Goal Setting

Purpose:

A. To identify and discuss steps to goal setting.

Hints and Procedures:

Provide the members with the handouts. Discuss concepts of self-determination, commitment, persistence, and priorities to support the achievement of goals. Ask a member to participate as a volunteer in a role-playing activity. Use the ten steps for the role-playing activity. Promote the group discussion by using each of the ten steps to goal setting.

Group Session Model:

The group session was aimed at identifying and discussing steps to goal setting. The members were provided with handouts containing ten steps to goal setting. They were asked to review their needs of goal setting and use the ten manageable steps to achieve their goals. Also, concepts, such as being realistic, committed, and persistent, were discussed as valuable steps to support the achievement of goals.

The patient appeared slightly disheveled and acted somewhat agitated. He responded to internal stimulus with ruminative thinking and made delusional statements. The patient recognized his need to identify attainable goals as one of the first steps to goal setting. He stated, "Well, of course, I want to be realistic, and one of my goals is to start my own business. I am a car mechanic, and I worked as a mechanic before, so I want to open my own business."

The clinician discussed with the patient the tendency of people to set unrealistic and unattainable goals, leading to discouragement and the inability to achieve them. The patient supported this discussion and continued to state that his goal would be realistic and attainable.

The staff has suggested that the patient will need to continue attending and receiving treatment at this level of service to prevent any possible exacerbation of his mental illness symptoms.

Topic 1: Learning Principles to Goal Setting

Exercise 2: Steps to Goal Setting

The impact of goal setting in a person's life would greatly improve the quality of life of that person. However, the process of goal setting may require a combination of steps including concepts, knowledge, motivation, and action.

- **The Ten Steps to Goal Setting**

    1. Think about one attainable goal in your life.
    2. Ask why you need to develop this goal.
    3. Ask how this goal would improve the quality of your life.
    4. Ask how you can motivate yourself to achieve this goal.
    5. Identify at least two ways to implement this goal.
    6. Identify at least two concepts to support the achievement of this goal.
    7. Ask what should be the first manageable step to achieve this goal.
    8. Ask what should be the second manageable step to achieve this goal.
    9. Identify potential obstacles to attaining this goal.
    10. Ask how you can overcome these obstacles to attain this goal.

Topic 1: Learning Principles to Goal Setting

Exercise 3: Wishes

Purpose:

    A. To explore wishes as a guide to identify potential personal goals.

Hints and Procedures:

    Distribute the handouts provided below. Review the concepts of the realistic versus the unrealistic in the achievement of goals. Use the questions and ask the members to think about their wishes in a time period (e.g., what would they like doing daily?). Encourage the members to focus on their realistic wishes as a guide to develop personal goals.

Group Session Model:

    The group session was led to encourage the members to divulge personal information and wishes as a guide to identify potential personal goals. To facilitate the group activity and discussion, the members were asked to use handouts with questions related to wishes that could be granted within some period of time (e.g., daily, weekly). The members were asked to explore their wishes and whether or not they could be realistic and attainable goals.

    The patient's depressive mood continued throughout the session consistent with his anxious affect, sad facial expression, rigid posture, and isolation. The patient was able to participate in the group discussion upon prompting. The patient stated, "One of my wishes is to feel better about myself." Then the patient added, "I would wish to go out weekly."

    The members empathized with the patient concerning his wish and recognized it as being realistic. Also, the patient was encouraged to answer other questions related to wishes as a guide to goal formation. He was receptive to the encouragement.

    The staff will continue to provide the patient with the opportunity to explore other personal wishes and stimulate his development of realistic goals to meet his personal needs.

Topic 1: Learning Principles to Goal Setting

Exercise 3: Wishes

My Great Wishes in Life

Your wishes may assist you in the development of personal goals. They may work as a guide in the process of developing your goals. Many of the great achievements and inventions in our world started out as wishes first.

- What are your wishes?

    1. What would you wish to do here in this group?
    2. What is the most important wish in your life? Why?
    3. What would you wish to do daily?
    4. What would you wish to do weekly?
    5. What would you wish to do monthly?
    6. What would you wish to do annually?
    7. What would you wish to do in five years from now?
    8. Are your wishes above realistic? Why do you think so?
    9. How can you make your wishes come true?
    10. Are any of your wishes coming true here? Explain.

Topic 1: Learning Principles to Goal Setting

Exercise 4: Purpose and Direction

Purpose:

    A. To identify realistic goals that give purpose and direction in life.
    B. To increase goal utilization in life.

Hints and Procedures:

Warm up the group discussion with this analogy: "Goal utilization is like a map to give life purpose and direction." Distribute the handouts provided below, and encourage the members to answer the questions related to goal utilization.

Group Session Model:

This group session consisted of increasing daily goal utilization as a map to give life purpose and direction. The clinician established rapport by providing examples of purpose in his own life. Then each member was prompted to use handouts containing questions to help him or her identify goals that can give him or her purpose and direction in life.

The patient was still exhibiting a moderate level of depression as evidenced by a sad affect, initial guarded behavior, and apparent tiredness. However, the patient demonstrated interest in the topic. He was attentive, offered positive feedback to other members, and was responsive to moderate prompting. The patient commented, "I have always set goals in my life, except now when I have not been able to accomplish my goals because of my depression." Also, the patient added, "Knowing that I must come here every day has been giving me a sense of purpose and direction to help me learn how to deal with my symptoms."

The therapeutic means consisted of providing the members with education, encouragement, support, and reassurance. The patient was receptive to the therapeutic intervention.

The future sessions will continue to encourage the patient to get engaged in the group discussion in order to facilitate the therapeutic process and prevent further exacerbation of his mental illness symptoms.

Topic 1: Learning Principles to Goal Setting

Exercise 4: Purpose and Direction

Goal utilization should be a continuous life skill to be used on a daily basis. It gives us purpose and direction in life. When we start our day knowing what we are going to do, the day may seem more productive. We should think about where we are going.

- Our goal utilization should be like a map to give us the exact direction. Think about this for a moment and answer at least one question below.

    1. What do you plan to achieve in your life?
    2. Why are you coming to this group?
    3. What do you plan to do when you leave this group?
    4. Can you identify at least two daily goals that will give you direction?
    5. Can you identify at least one weekly goal that will give you direction?
    6. Can you identify at least one monthly goal that will give you direction?
    7. What do you expect to achieve six months from now?
    8. What else would give you purpose and direction in life?
    9. What happens when a person does not know what to do in life?
    10. What can we do to help a person who is lost in life?

Topic 1: Learning Principles to Goal Setting

Exercise 5: Realistic versus Unrealistic

Purpose:

    A. To implement realistic and attainable goals.
    B. To identify the differences between realistic and unrealistic goals.

Hints and Procedures:

While the handouts are being passed out, review the concept of goals and their benefits. Promote the group discussion by using each true-or-false statement on realistic versus unrealistic goals. Focus the group discussion on the implementation of realistic goals.

Group Session Model:

The focus of this group session was to help the members to implement realistic goals. The clinician warmed up the group discussion by reviewing some concepts and benefits of goal setting. The members were provided with handouts with true-or-false statements related to realistic and unrealistic goals. The group discussion focused on the content of each statement with emphasis on the implementation of realistic goals.

The patient's affect was blunted, and his mood was dysphoric. He was observed as anxious and apprehensive. Although the patient was hesitant in his responses, he was able to follow the group discussion and grasped the above concepts related to realistic and unrealistic goals. The patient stated, "My goal here is to complete this program and to remain free from drug addiction."

The clinician provided the patient with positive feedback and supportive counseling, to which the patient reacted in a positive way. The patient increased his understanding about the importance of maintaining self-confidence and self-control, some of the benefits discussed during the group discussion about setting realistic goals.

The future interventions will continue to encourage the patient's realistic goal attainment as part of the process to help him reach mood stabilization.

Topic 1: Learning Principles to Goal Setting

Exercise 5: Realistic versus Unrealistic

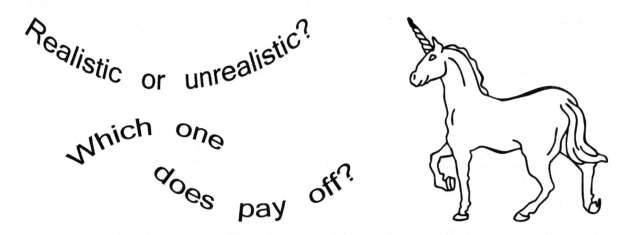

Realistic or unrealistic? Which one does pay off?

One of the most important steps to goal setting is to determine which goals are realistic and which are unrealistic. This process may not be easy since what would be realistic for one person may not be realistic for another one and vice versa.

- Why should we develop goals?[1]

- Which statements below are true (T) and which are false (F)?[2]

		T or F?
1.	Setting realistic goals is the best way to get excited about possibilities.	( )
2.	Being realistic or unrealistic encourages positive permanent lifestyle changes.	( )
3.	Goals are realistic if they are conducive to your life.	( )
4.	In order to reach realistic or unrealistic goals, you need to make some changes.	( )
5.	If the goals reflect your true desires, they may be realistic.	( )
6.	The action will never take place if your realistic goals are too specific.	( )
7.	You can only achieve a realistic goal if your intention turns into action.	( )
8.	Setting unrealistic goals is not the main reason why people fail.	( )
9.	Nothing can happen without the implementation of realistic goals.	( )
10.	You should always ask someone else to make sure your goals are right for you.	( )
11.	If you set realistic goals, you will save yourself a lot of time.	( )
12.	Your goals will direct your life according to your dreams and possessions.	( )

---

[1] They may help us maintain self-confidence and self-control. Also, they may help us decrease symptoms, reach stabilization, and prevent relapse.

[2] Answer key: 1) True, 2) False, 3) True, 4) False, 5) True, 6) False, 7) True, 8) False, 9) True, 10) False, 11) True, 12) False.

Topic 2: Making Goals to Work on Symptoms

Exercise 1: Motivating Goals

Purpose:

    A. To increase motivation to achieve goals.

Hints and Procedures:

    Discuss with the members the concept "your motivation is not coming from the sky and is not coming from under your door" as a simple means of explaining that motivation must come from within. Distribute the handouts provided below, and encourage the group discussion about how to use the attached strategies to increase motivation to achieve goals.

Group Session Model:

    The group session was focused on assisting the members to increase motivation to achieve goals. The concept "your motivation is not coming from the sky and is not coming from under your door" was initially discussed among the members as a simple means of explaining that motivation must come from within. The members began to understand how they must be self-motivated. Then they were given handouts with strategies to increase motivation to achieve goals and were encouraged to discuss how to use them.

    The patient came to the group session speaking in a halting manner and with a predominant anxious mood. The patient was observed with a tense posture, had difficulty staying still, and had difficulty concentrating. The patient was able to discuss with the members one strategy to increase motivation to achieve goals. The patient stated, "I have been trying to be more committed to the treatment, especially coming here every day. As a result, this has helped me to increase my motivation, and in turn, develop important goals."

    Positive feedback was provided by the members regarding the patient's use of the strategy of being committed to increase goal motivation. The patient responded positively to the feedback. Also, he was attentive to the group discussion about many other techniques to increase his motivation to achieve goals, such as establishing habits, recognizing self-expression, and improving his positive attitude.

    The professional team has determined that the patient continues to need this level of service in order to implement personal goals, decrease his mental illness symptoms, and increase his level of functioning.

Topic 2: Making Goals to Work on Symptoms

Exercise 1: Motivating Goals

The success of achieving goals would depend on your level of motivation. People fail to achieve their goals because their levels of motivation are low. There are some helpful strategies that can help you increase motivation to achieve goals. But the thing is that *your motivation is not coming from the sky and is not coming from under your door.* You have to look for it, and you have to work hard to get it.

- How can you use the strategies below to increase motivation?

    1. Self-determination: _____
    2. Self-respect: _____
    3. Recognition of self-expression: _____
    4. Establishment of habits: _____
    5. Development of disciplines: _____
    6. Positive attitude: _____
    7. Consistence: _____
    8. Persistence: _____
    9. Commitment: _____
    10. Hard work: _____

Topic 2: Making Goals to Work on Symptoms

Exercise 2: Decreasing Symptoms

Purpose:

    A. To identify and develop goals to decrease symptoms.
    B. To develop personal goals to improve daily functioning.

Hints and Procedures:

While the handouts are being distributed, initiate the group discussion by pointing out that making positive goals is psychologically healthy. Review the members' mental illness symptoms and challenge each member to identify at least one symptom to be discussed during the group session. Assist each member in identifying realistic goals to decrease his or her symptoms.

Group Session Model:

The group session focused on identifying and developing goals to decrease mental illness symptoms. The clinician initiated the group discussion by pointing out that making positive goals is psychologically healthy. The members were asked to use handouts with a list of several mental illness symptoms and identify corresponding goals to decrease them.

The patient has regularly indicated an anxious affect, paranoid mood, suspicion, and apprehensive behaviors. The patient stated, "When I become paranoid, I still try to function on my own and keep a steady pace." The patient continued with his idea by saying, "Two of my goals are to learn more about my paranoia and improve my social support system."

The members supported and encouraged the patient to continue improving his support system as a valuable goal to cope with paranoia, to which the patient was receptive. The patient demonstrated greater insight into other remaining areas of choice on which he needs to continue working.

The clinician will continue to assist the patient to build recognition and sensitivity to mental illness symptoms, and to develop goals to decrease his mental illness symptoms.

Topic 2: Making Goals to Work on Symptoms

Exercise 2: Decreasing Symptoms

Symptoms and Goals
what are your symptoms?
What are your goals?

Knowing about your mental illness symptoms should be one of the first steps in developing goals to cope with them. The development of goals should be an ongoing, daily process to cope with your symptoms. Making positive goals is psychologically healthy.

- Identify one of your mental illness symptoms below:

  ☐ 1. Sleep disturbances ☐ 6. Appetite disturbances
  ☐ 2. Increased anxiety ☐ 7. Hopelessness/helplessness
  ☐ 3. Isolation ☐ 8. Psychotic symptoms (identify)
  ☐ 4. Lack of motivation ☐ 9. Negative thoughts
  ☐ 5. Withdrawal ☐ 10. Other _____

- Identify at least two goals to cope with this symptom.

  In order to cope with symptom number (   ) above, I can develop the following:

  Goal 1: _____
  Goal 2: _____

Topic 2: Making Goals to Work on Symptoms

Exercise 3: Activities and Goals

Purpose:

    A. To develop goals to decrease mental illness symptoms.
    B. To explore goals for leisure activities.

Hints and Procedures:

Distribute the handouts provided below, and read the text about activities and goals. Review concepts of commitment, frequency, time, quantity, persistence, and others related to goal formation and goal achievement. Encourage each member to use the exercise to form and achieve their goals to meet personal needs and decrease their mental illness symptoms. Assist and train the members to convert activities into goals by following the model provided.

Group Session Model:

The clinician introduced the topic of goals by reviewing with the members important concepts related to goal formation. Then the members were encouraged to use handouts in order to practice the conversion of activities into realistic goals including concepts, such as commitment, frequency, time, and quantity.

The patient had an initial evasive eye contact and downcast facial expression, and was withdrawn and guarded. However, as the session progressed, the patient became a bit more involved when directly approached. The patient stated, "I would like to practice positive thinking. I feel that it would help me gain more confidence in myself."

The patient was assisted by the clinician and the members in converting positive thinking into a goal. For instance, it was suggested to the patient that he start using positive thinking daily for at least five minutes, three times a day. The patient increased his understanding of the concept "converting activities into goals" and agreed on its importance to decrease his mental illness symptoms and reach his mood stabilization.

The staff will continue to assist and encourage the patient to develop goals to meet his personal needs as part of the process to help him reach his mood stabilization.

Topic 2: Making Goals to Work on Symptoms

Exercise 3: Activities and Goals

What have been your personal activities and goals in life?

Exploring personal activities, especially the leisure ones, and goals should be part of your entire life. Also, they should be part of your treatment process as well. An activity does not necessarily mean a goal. It needs to be elaborated and converted into a goal and needs to be specific. How? You are going to be trained today to do that.

- Let's think about a physical routine activity. For instance, walking to increase one's sleeping pattern may be a routine or daily activity. But, walking is only an activity, not a goal yet. It needs some ingredients to convert it into a goal. They may include commitment, frequency, time, and quantity, among others. So, let's convert walking, a physical activity, and other activities below into goals:

Activity	/Commitment	/Frequency	/Time	/Quantity
Physical:	I am going to walk	daily	in the afternoon	for thirty minutes
Recreational:				
Social:				
Spiritual:				
Mental:				
Intellectual:				

Topic 2: Making Goals to Work on Symptoms

Exercise 4: Instilling Hope

Purpose:

    A. To develop positive and realistic goals to instill hope.

Hints and Procedures:

Provide the members with the handouts, and start the group discussion about the importance of instilling hope. Ask the members for ideas of how to instill hope in life. Encourage the members to make resolutions and stimulate them to set goals as a process for their entire lives.

Group Session Model:

The group session was developed in order to encourage the members to develop positive and realistic goals to instill hope. The members were provided with handouts with information about instilling hope and a list of several realistic and positive goals. The members were asked to identify their ongoing realistic and positive goals from the list that might instill hope.

In the session, the patient was depressed. He was initially isolated from his peers, with a guarded and nonspontaneous behavior. Also, he showed a lack of motivation. However, the patient had no difficulty coming up with one of his realistic goals that he has been trying to implement in order to cope with his isolation. The patient commented, "One of my goals from now on is to make new friends. Since I became depressed, I isolated myself too much, and now I feel very lonely."

Positive feedback was provided by the members regarding the patient's ongoing goal, to which he was receptive. Also, during the course of the group discussion, the patient was attentive to the importance of making resolutions and continues setting goals throughout his entire life.

The staff will continue to encourage the patient's achievement of positive and realistic goals to instill hope as part of the process to help him stabilize his mood.

158 ■ *Group Goals*

Topic 2: Making Goals to Work on Symptoms

Exercise 4: Instilling Hope

Thinking about realistic goals that can improve your life is an effective way of instilling hope. Life goes smoothly when you set realistic and positive goals, and when you know where you want to go. Hoping to accomplish something can make you feel good about yourself. You can start setting simple, realistic, and positive goals like the ones provided here. But, remember! It is important that you continue with this process during your entire life.

- What has been one of your ongoing realistic and positive goals?

    ☐ 1. I am improving my sleeping pattern.
    ☐ 2. I am improving my abilities to concentrate.
    ☐ 3. I am making new friends.
    ☐ 4. I am increasing my motivation.
    ☐ 5. I am participating in recreational activities.
    ☐ 6. I am participating in social activities.
    ☐ 7. I am participating in spiritual activities.
    ☐ 8. I am working on my twelve-step program.
    ☐ 9. I am working on my grief steps.
    ☐ 10. I am decreasing my stress.
    ☐ 11. I am decreasing my anxiety.
    ☐ 12. I am decreasing my isolation.
    ☐ 13. I am decreasing my sadness.
    ☐ 14. Other _____

    ✧ How are you achieving this goal?

Topic 2: Making Goals to Work on Symptoms

Exercise 5: Long-Term and Short-Term Goals

Purpose:

    A. To establish long-term and short-term goals.

Hints and Procedures:

Distribute the handouts provided below, and ask the members to define long-term and short-term goals. Use the true-or-false statements to promote the group discussion about long-term and short-term goals. Ask the members to identify short-term goals to decrease their mental illness symptoms. Discuss long-term goals, such as living a more independent life, starting work, and going back to school.

Group Session Model:

The group session focused on assisting the members in establishing short-term and long-term goals related to their treatment plans in order to facilitate their psychiatric stabilization while the further escalation of symptoms is prevented. The members were provided with handouts with true-or-false statements related to long-term and short-term goals. Each member was asked to come up with one current short-term goal to decrease his or her mental illness symptoms. Also, the members were asked to think about long-term goals, such as living a more independent life and starting work.

The patient was sad and tearful in this group session while recalling the recent loss of his three-year-old son. His level of energy was low, and he needed to be encouraged to participate in the group discussion. The clinician encouraged the patient to verbalize his short-term goal supporting his stabilization. He stated, "I suffer from depression, and one of my current short-term goals is to learn what to do to feel better." Also, the patient verbalized one of his current long-term goals by saying, "I want to live on my own in the future."

The patient received support and encouragement from his peers concerning his ongoing goals. The patient was receptive to the support received.

The professional team has suggested that the patient will continue to need to attend this level of service in order to work on the achievement of his long-term and short-term goals supporting his stabilization of mood.

Topic 2: Making Goals to Work on Symptoms

Exercise 5: Long-Term and Short-Term Goals

When setting personal goals, it is important to set both long-term and short-term goals in order to achieve what we want to achieve. Often, long-term goals are our most meaningful and important goals. So, let's learn more about this important subject today.

- Please use "T" for true and "F" for false for the statements below:[1]

    (   ) 1. Your personal goal setting needs to begin by looking at your long-term goals.
    (   ) 2. The achievement of short-term goals is usually far in the future.
    (   ) 3. Long-term goals are very necessary, but it may be very easy to become discouraged.
    (   ) 4. Long-term and short-term goals are the same as wishes and dreams.
    (   ) 5. The way to achieve the most out of your goals is to first set your long-term goals.
    (   ) 6. If you just set short-term goals, you may put them off in the future for some reason.
    (   ) 7. Short-term goals are needed to be made to support existing long-term goals.
    (   ) 8. Long-term goals can be set by analyzing your short-term goals.
    (   ) 9. By setting long-term goals, you have a vision of what you ultimately want to achieve.
    (   ) 10. One of your short-term goals here should include an immediate job position.
    (   ) 11. One of your long-term goals should be to live an independent life.
    (   ) 12. The decrease of mental illness symptoms is best reached through long-term goals.

    ✧ Why do you think your statements above are true or false?

    ✧ Can you identify at least three short-term goals to decrease symptoms?

---

[1] Answer key: 1) True, 2) False, 3) True, 4) False, 5) True, 6) False, 7) True, 8) False, 9) True, 10) False, 11) True, 12) False.

Topic 2: Making Goals to Work on Symptoms

Exercise 6: Goal Commitment

Purpose:

    A. To make a personal commitment with goal utilization.

Hints and Procedures:

    While the handouts are being distributed, review with the members the concept of goal commitment by discussing the following: "If there is no evidence that you are committed to achieving a goal, you should delete it from your list." Challenge each member to use the command *"I will..."* to make a commitment to goal utilization.

Group Session Model:

    The objective of this group session was aimed at reinforcing the members' personal commitment to goal utilization. The clinician highlighted that goal commitment should be an essential part of one's daily life to progress, as well as to decrease mental illness symptoms. The members were provided with handouts with a list of several "I will ..." commands for goal commitment. The members were asked to use the commands to write their personal goals.

    The patient came to the group session neat and clean, but seemed depressed and anxious as evidenced by his tense posture, sad affect, and initial withdrawn behavior. However, the patient was able to relate to peers and selected one goal commitment. The patient commented, "Today, I will start walking to help me sleep better."

    The members supported the patient's goal commitment. The patient was receptive to the support received. He discussed with the group his understanding of why making this commitment to his personal goal utilization is important in his life.

    The professional team will continue to encourage the patient to incorporate realistic personal goal utilization to increase his sense of productivity and facilitate the process of his stabilization.

Topic 2: Making Goals to Work on Symptoms

Exercise 6: Goal Commitment

Goal commitment should be part of our daily lives. You cannot go far in your life unless you know where to go and are committed to your goals. Goal commitments are essential to your progress and should be part of your stabilization process. So, let's write some goals you might want to incorporate in your life.

- Please use the commands below to write one of your goals.

    1. Now, I will _____
    2. Today, I will _____
    3. Tomorrow, I will _____
    4. Next week, I will _____
    5. Next month, I will _____
    6. When I finish the program, I will _____
    7. Six months from now, I will _____
    8. Next year, I will _____
    9. Five years from now, I will _____
    10. I always will _____

    ✧ How can you implement this goal?

    ✧ How can you commit yourself to this goal?

Topic 3: Monitoring Progress on Goals

Exercise 1: Master Treatment Plan

Purpose:

    A. To discuss progress on goals from the master treatment plan.

Hints and Procedures:

    Distribute the handouts provided below. Read the material, and initiate the group discussion by educating the members about the master treatment plan. Provide the members with information or copies of their master treatment plans, including their problems, goals, and objectives. Encourage each member to select one personal problem, one goal, and at least one objective from the master treatment plan. Discuss the progress being made, provide positive feedback and support, and discuss any difficulty encountered in the process of meeting their goals and objectives.

Group Session Model:

    The group session was developed in order to discuss the members' ongoing progress from their master treatment plans. To facilitate the group discussion, the clinician provided the members with handouts with information related to a master treatment plan. Also, the members were given copies of their master treatment plans. Each member was encouraged to select one personal problem, one goal, and at least one objective from his or her master treatment plan to discuss during the group session. The group examined and addressed progress or problems related to each patient's treatment goals.

    The patient was agitated, restless, and anxious; fidgeted constantly; and spoke in a halting manner. Upon moderate prompting, the patient became involved in the group discussion. He spoke about his ineffective coping skills as one of his problems from his master treatment plan. The patient stated, "My goal to solve this problem is to learn coping skills to prevent relapse." The patient continued with his idea as follows: "I am working on objective number one, which requires me to develop at least three drug relapse prevention skills within the next two weeks."

    The staff praised the patient's progress and encouraged the patient to continue working on meeting his goals. The patient responded positively to the praise and encouragement.

    The staff will continue to assist and encourage the patient to meet goals from his master treatment plan in order to stabilize his mood and affect.

Topic 3: Monitoring Progress on Goals

Exercise 1: Master Treatment Plan

The success of your treatment depends on your ability to meet goals and objectives from your master treatment plan. A master treatment plan is where we have written your problems, goals, and objectives to help you cope with your problems and eliminate or significantly reduce your mental illness symptoms. Goals are developed to address your problems, and objectives are developed to meet your goals. Your objectives are intended to eliminate or decrease your mental illness symptoms. Today, we are going to discuss the progress that you have been making toward meeting goals and objectives from your master treatment plan. The main part of your master treatment plan consists of the following components: problems, goals, and objectives.

- From your master treatment plan, try to complete the following statements:

    ♦ One of my current problems is
    _____

    ♦ One of my current goals to solve this problem is
    _____

    ♦ One of my current objectives to meet this goal is
    _____

    ♦ I have been meeting this objective by
    _____

Topic 3: Monitoring Progress on Goals

Exercise 2: Obstacles to Goal Attainment

Purpose:

    A. To identify obstacles to goal attainment.

Hints and Procedures:

    While the handouts are being passed out, start reading the text information and warm up the group discussion by asking the members this question: "What would be the most difficult obstacle to goal attainment?" Use the brainstorming technique to encourage the members to answer the above question. Encourage the members to identify any direct or indirect obstacles to their current goals' attainment, as well as to discuss how to overcome the obstacles.

Group Session Model:

    The group session's purpose was to identify obstacles to goal attainment. The clinician provided the members with handouts with a list of several possible obstacles to goal attainment. The group session started with this question: "What would be the most difficulty obstacle to goal attainment?" Then the members were encouraged to identify any direct or indirect obstacles they have been encountering in attaining their current goals.

    As in the prior sessions, the patient was isolated, somewhat suspicious, depressed, and sad. His sad affect was congruent with his depressed mood. His participation was limited to direct approaches. The patient stated, "Doubts, fears, and lack of patience have been some of the barriers to achieving my goals."

    The patient's barriers were recognized by his peers as typical obstacles to goal attainment. Also, the members discussed other obstacles to goal attainment—including lack of freedom, poor coping skills, and a poor support system—as having a direct impact on attaining goals. The patient concurred with these obstacles.

    The further therapeutic interventions will continue to focus on the patient's ongoing goals to decrease his mental illness symptoms and improve his daily level of functioning.

Topic 3: Monitoring Progress on Goals

Exercise 2: Obstacles to Goal Attainment

What have been the pitfalls and barriers for your goal attainment?

The attainment of goals in our lives may be faced with barriers and pitfalls. They might include fears, self-doubt, negative thought pattterns that are highly resistant to changes, and interpersonal conflict, among others.[1] So, it is important to know about these typical barriers and pitfalls to goal attainment.

- In the list below, you are going to find many obstacles to goal attainment. Label those obstacles that you can change and deal with by yourself by using the acronym "CBC" (can be changed), and label those for which you would require outside help by using the acronym "ROH" (require outside help).

    (____) 1. Lack of freedom
    (____) 3. Lack of planning
    (____) 4. Lack of persistence
    (____) 5. Lack of knowledge
    (____) 6. Lack of motivation
    (____) 7. Lack of insight
    (____) 8. Lack of financial resources
    (____) 9. Difficulty concentrating
    (____) 10. Lack of time management skills
    (____) 12. Lack of commitment
    (____) 13. Lack of consistency
    (____) 14. Lack of listening skills
    (____) 15. Lack of patience
    (____) 16. Lack of support
    (____) 17. Dysfunctional family
    (____) 18. Other _____

  ✧ How can you work on the obstacles CBC and ROH above?

---

[1] Our fears are probably the most difficult obstacle to goal attainment.

Topic 3: Monitoring Progress on Goals

Exercise 3: Ongoing Progress

Purpose:

A. To monitor ongoing progress in the achievement of goals.

Hints and Procedures:

Distribute the handouts provided below, and encourage the members to review their ongoing progress in the achievement of goals to meet their life needs. In order to support the group discussion on the achievement of goals, review key concepts of goal achievement, such as the idea that goals should be realistic, attainable, specific, and measurable. Also, the review should include the concepts of quantity and time.

Group Session Model:

The group session focused on helping the members to review their ongoing progress on the achievement of goals. The members were given handouts with a list of several areas of life needs and were encouraged to identify areas in which they have been noting progress during their participation in the group sessions.

During the session, the patient was anhedonic and tearful, and exhibited sadness in his facial expression suggesting a dominant depressive mental status. Upon being prompted by the clinician, the patient was able to identify one area and one corresponding goal he has been making progress on. He stated, "I have been trying to set spiritual goals to improve my inner peace. So, I started attending church every Sunday."

The members provided the patient with support and encouragement. The patient recognized the need to make a consistent effort to work on setting goals and make progress in other areas of his life as discussed by the members.

The patient has frequently demonstrated impaired coping mechanisms and a poor level of functioning. So, the staff has recommended that the patient continue this level of service to prevent an inpatient psychiatric hospitalization.

Topic 3: Monitoring Progress on Goals

Exercise 3: Ongoing Progress

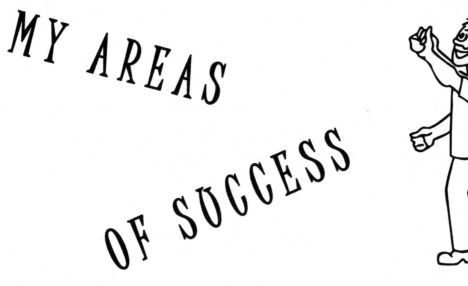

The achievement of goals should be a daily ongoing process to meet life needs in many areas, including the following: psychological, emotional, social, spiritual, intellectual, and professional. Also, the goals should help improve the following: self-esteem, inner peace, everyday functioning, and physical appearance. There are a variety of goals that should be set to meet such needs. So, it is important to monitor your ongoing progress on goals in these areas.

- Please identify at least one goal that you have been working on to meet your needs in the following areas:

    1. Mental: _____
    2. Physiological: _____
    3. Social: _____
    4. Intellectual: _____
    5. Professional: _____
    6. Spiritual: _____
    7. Inner peace: _____
    8. Self-esteem: _____
    9. Functional: _____
    10. Other _____

    ✧ I have been meeting this goal by _____

Topic 4: Assessing Achievement of Goals

Exercise 1: Getting Ready for Discharge

Purpose:

    A. To develop an appropriate aftercare discharge plan.
    B. To discuss an aftercare discharge plan.

Hints and Procedures:

Distribute the handouts provided below, and encourage the members to answer the questions regarding their aftercare discharge plans. Review the importance of developing a concrete aftercare discharge plan, which might include constructive projects, continuance of goal setting, and the use of support and social groups to aid in recovery. Talk about social clubs, senior citizens' centers, clubs of friends, and activities including writing, painting, making phone calls, etc. Ask this question: "What should be included in an effective aftercare discharge plan?" (See suggestions in the handout footnote.) Also, make a list of what should be included in an effective discharge plan using the group's input.

Group Session Model:

The purpose of this group session was to assist and encourage the members to develop appropriate aftercare discharge plans. The clinician initiated the group discussion by reviewing the importance of developing a concrete aftercare discharge plan, which might include constructive projects and the continuance of goal setting, among others. The members were asked to use handouts and answer questions related to their own aftercare discharge plans. The group discussion focused on this question: "What should be included in an effective aftercare discharge plan?"

The patient was observed as being isolated, having a sad affect, and often making pessimistic comments. He had a hostile and oppositional demeanor at times. The patient was redirected and encouraged to participate in the group discussion. The patient stated, "For me, attending NA meetings is one of the activities that I should include in my aftercare discharge plan."

The members provided the patient with support and reinforcement. Also, the patient had an opportunity to review many other goals that should be part of an effective aftercare discharge plan, including the following: complying with medication, continued follow-ups with a psychiatrist, use of leisure time, and social outlets. He seemed to concur with these goals as well.

The future sessions will continue to assist and encourage the patient to develop appropriate goals for his aftercare discharge plan.

Topic 4: Assessing Achievement of Goals

Exercise 1: Getting Ready for Discharge

Are you ready for discharge?

Understanding the concept of "getting ready for discharge" is vitally important. Individuals are at a significant risk for relapse in the future if they have poor insight about what to do after being discharged from this program.

- Are you ready for discharge?

- Choose at least one question below to discuss with your peers.

    1. When should you start your aftercare discharge plan? Why?
    2. Why is it important to have a concrete aftercare discharge plan?
    3. What are specific improvements you have made in the program?
    4. What have you learned in the groups to prevent you from relapsing?
    5. When should you be ready for discharge?
    6. What do you need to do when you are getting ready for discharge?
    7. What should be included in an effective aftercare discharge plan?[1]
    8. How can you continue to make improvements?
    9. What is your plan to increase your activity level upon discharge?
    10. How are you going to continue to manage your mental illness after leaving the program?

---

[1] It should include medication compliance, continued follow-up with the psychiatrist, use of leisure time, social outlets, NA/AA meetings, church attendance, nutrition, relaxation, and physical exercises.

Topic 4: Assessing Achievement of Goals

Exercise 2: Present and Future Goals

Purpose:

    A. To discuss achievement of present and future goals.
    B. To share concerns about the future.

Hints and Procedures:

Review the concepts of positive expectations and purpose in life as they relate to goal setting. Distribute the handouts provided below, and encourage the members to discuss the achievement of their present and future goals.

Group Session Model:

The group session focused on discussing the achievement of present and future goals. The clinician reviewed with the members concepts of positive expectations and purpose in life as they related to goal setting. Then the members were asked to use handouts and answer questions related to their present and future goal achievement, as well as their concerns about the future.

The patient has regularly showed a dominant depressed mood congruent with his blunted affect. The patient was observed as angry, and at times, with an increased anxiety as he was easily annoyed. With hesitation, the patient explained to the group, "My concern about the future is how to continue to be stable. I have achieved many goals here, but I still need to achieve goals to help me control my anger."

The members assisted the patient by reviewing some goals to control anger, including the use of daily cognitive restructuring techniques, praying, and relaxation. The patient responded positively to the group support and recommendations. The members continued to discuss and share other goals and concerns about the future, such as how to prevent a relapse of mental illness and how to develop a more independent life. The patient was attentive to the discussion.

The staff has recommended the patient continue treatment to achieve his goals, reduce his symptoms of mental illness to a more manageable level, and start preparations for his upcoming discharge.

Topic 4: Assessing Achievement of Goals

Exercise 2: Present and Future Goals

Creating positive expectations for the future and giving purpose to life is done only through the achievement of goals. So, it is important to think of your present and future goal achievement.

- Goal achievement:

    1. Can you identity at least two goals that give you purpose in life?

    2. What goals have you been achieving in this group?

    3. What goals do you still want to achieve in this group? Why?

    4. What are your expectations for the future?

    5. What are your concerns about the future? Why?

PART VII

GROUP INSIGHT

TOPICS 1–4

WITH

TWENTY EXERCISES

Topic 1: Understanding How Treatment Can Help

Exercise 1: Treatment Expectations

Purpose:

    A. To identify reasons to be in treatment.
    B. To discuss the benefits of treatment.
    C. To explore patients' expectations of treatment.

Hints and Procedures:

Use the handouts provided below to promote the group discussion about the members' reasons to be in treatment, expectations of treatment, attitudes toward treatment, and benefits of treatment. Brainstorm all the positives of treatment, such as why a person should be proactive and participate in the group psychotherapy sessions.

Group Session Model:

The group session focused on exploring the members' expectations of treatment. The members were given handouts with questions to promote the group discussion about their reasons to be in treatment, expectations of treatment, attitudes toward treatment, and benefits of treatment.

During the session, the patient was observed to be depressed as shown by his poor eye contact, guarded demeanor, sad facial expression, and teary eyes. However, the patient was alert and verbally interactive. The patient commented, "I believe the treatment is going to help me learn how to keep myself stable."

The clinician provided the patient with positive feedback and reinforcement. The patient was encouraged to continue to be proactive in treatment to maintain gains and accomplish all of the treatment goals. Also, the members identified many ways treatment has been helping them to learn new behaviors, concepts, values, and combined treatments to reach stabilization. The patient was open to suggestions and demonstrated an understanding of the new information obtained.

The professional team will continue to assist and encourage the patient to be proactive with his treatment as part of the process to reach his mood stabilization.

Topic 1: Understanding How Treatment Can Help

Exercise 1: Treatment Expectations

What should be the true reasons to be here?

People may have different reasons, expectations, and attitudes when they come to the group psychotherapy sessions. Group psychotherapy is a kind of treatment to treat mental illness, including alcohol and drug addiction. People's expectations, reasons, and attitudes may be realistic or unrealistic, and they can be positive or negative. How are yours?

- Please answer at least one question below.

  1. Do you know the reasons why you are in this group psychotherapy?
  2. Do you know why the question above should be the first question you must answer?
  3. Is your attitude toward your treatment positive or negative? Why?
  4. What are the benefits of the treatment?
  5. If you cannot think about any benefits, why not?
  6. Can people change their attitudes? How? Why?
  7. What do you expect to achieve in this group?
  8. What should you do in this group psychotherapy? What shouldn't you do? Why?
  9. How can treatment help you achieve that?
  10. Why should you be proactive while in this program?

Topic 1: Understanding How Treatment Can Help

Exercise 2: Self-Responsibility

Purpose:

    A. To increase self-responsibility for treatment.

Hints and Procedures:

Start the group discussion by reviewing with the members the concept of self-responsibility as related to treatment. By using handouts, encourage the members to discuss the involvement they should have in their treatment. Emphasize the members' roles and the active participation in the treatment process.

Group Session Model:

The objective of this group session was to assist and encourage the members to increase self-responsibility for their treatment. The group discussion started with a review of the concept "self-responsibility" as related to treatment. Then the members were encouraged to use handouts with statements about how much involvement they should have in their treatment.

The patient was observed as being isolated and withdrawn, having non-spontaneous speech, and being easily distracted. The clinician encouraged the patient to come up with at least one idea related to his self-responsibility for his treatment. In response to this intervention, the patient commented, "I understand that one of my responsibilities, especially here in this group, is to be cooperative."

Positive and supportive feedback were provided by the members regarding the patient's opinion. The patient was able to understand many other responsibilities for his own treatment discussed during the group discussion. Among them, the members discussed the importance of being active, acting aggressively toward relieving symptoms, and learning about one's diagnoses and prognoses.

The professional team will continue to assist the patient in increasing his functional level by increasing his self-responsibility for his treatment.

Topic 1: Understanding How Treatment Can Help

Exercise 2: Self-Responsibility

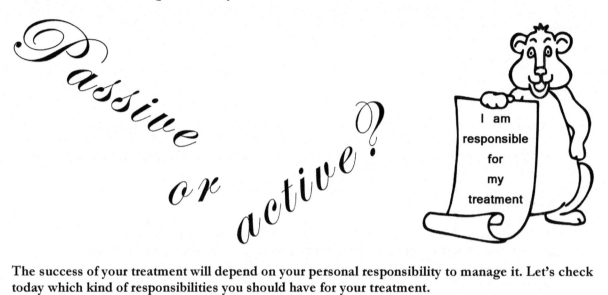

The success of your treatment will depend on your personal responsibility to manage it. Let's check today which kind of responsibilities you should have for your treatment.

- For each statement below related to your treatment, use (A) if you agree with its content or (D) if you disagree.

		A	D
1.	It is important to know about my diagnosis.	( )	( )
2.	It is important to know about my prognosis.	( )	( )
3.	I can get benefits from my treatment by being either passive or active.	( )	( )
4.	I should not self-disclose any personal information in this group.	( )	( )
5.	I believe that I should wait for the treatment to work.	( )	( )
6.	I should wait for my motivation to increase for the treatment to work.	( )	( )
7.	I just need to learn about my mental illness, and that's it!	( )	( )
8.	I need to act aggressively to relieve my symptoms.	( )	( )
9.	I need to remain cooperative.	( )	( )
10.	I need to continue with my treatment after leaving this group.	( )	( )

✧ Why do you agree or disagree with the statements above?

Topic 1: Understanding How Treatment Can Help

Exercise 3: "I Have Difficulty ..."

Purpose:

   A. To identify difficult treatment areas to work on.

Hints and Procedures:

Initiate the group discussion by reviewing concepts related to treatment (e.g., treatments without changes are not effective). Use the handouts provided below, and encourage each member to identify at least one difficult treatment area to work on for which they need help to produce effective changes. Encourage the members to complete this statement: "I have difficulty ..." Discuss alternatives on how to overcome their difficulties.

Group Session Model:

This group session focused on assisting the members in identifying areas related to their treatments in which they have been having difficulties in making progress and are in need of help to produce effective changes. In order to facilitate the group discussion, the members were encouraged to use handouts with a list of possible difficult treatment areas. Each member was encouraged to identify at least one difficult treatment area and complete this statement: "I have difficulty ..." Also, the members were encouraged to discuss alternatives on how to overcome their difficult treatment areas.

The patient has regularly indicated depression, which is best described by his sad facial expression, downcast eyes, rigid posture, and guarded behavior. The patient was receptive to minimum prompting and told the group, "I have difficulty expressing my needs."

The members assisted the patient in overcoming his difficulty expressing his needs by practicing assertiveness. The patient was receptive to the suggestions and seemed to be open to other members' comments related to other difficult treatment areas.

The staff has recommended that the patient continue the psychotherapy sessions to overcome his areas of difficulty in treatment.

178 ■ *Group Insight*

Topic 1: Understanding How Treatment Can Help

Exercise 3: "I Have Difficulty ..."

During the process of your treatment, you may be faced with difficulty with some specific areas you should work on. So, it is important to identify these areas in order to help you continue making progress.

- Choose one of the statements below that apply to you, or write your own, in order to identify areas in which you have been having difficulty making progress.

    1. I have difficulty making appropriate choices.
    2. I have difficulty making changes.
    3. I have difficulty exploring alternatives to cope with my symptoms.
    4. I have difficulty developing discipline.
    5. I have difficulty asking for help.
    6. I have difficulty expressing my own needs.
    7. I have difficulty recognizing my weaknesses.
    8. I have difficulty accepting feedback.
    9. I have difficulty understanding my treatment.
    10. Other _____

    ✧ How can you overcome your difficulty?

Topic 1: Understanding How Treatment Can Help

Exercise 4: Gears and Combined Treatments

Purpose:

A. To discuss alternative combined treatments to treat mental illness.

Hints and Procedures:

Warm up the group discussion with the analogy of "gears and combined treatments" as it relates to the success of treatment. Distribute the handouts provided below, and encourage the members to share the combined treatments they have been using to treat mental illness.

Group Session Model:

The objective of this group session was to discuss with the members alternative combined treatments to treat mental illness. The members were encouraged to share the combined treatments they have been using for their treatment. The clinician warmed up the group discussion by reviewing the analogy of "gears and combined treatments" as it relates to the success of the treatment. The analogy provided the members with a simple visual means of grasping the idea of interconnected parts working together. Combined treatments to treat mental illness are like gears, as the members could learn from the handouts containing a list of several combined treatments to treat mental illness.

The patient had a dominant depressive mental status. He was initially guarded, isolated, and withdrawn. Also, he had a sad facial expression and low energy level. The patient was receptive to minimal prompting and expressed himself by saying, "Well, I have learned that medication should be part of my treatment. But, besides taking my medication as prescribed by my psychiatrist, I have also been learning more about my mental disease and how to better cope with my symptoms."

The clinician and the members supported the patient's understanding of the benefits of the combined treatments to treat his mental illness. The patient agreed to broaden his combined treatments for the success of his treatment.

The staff will continue to assist the patient with further therapeutic interventions in order to broaden his combined treatments for the success of his treatment.

Topic 1: Understanding How Treatment Can Help

Exercise 4: Gears and Combined Treatments

What is the analogy between gears and combined treatments to treat mental illness? Like gears in an engine, combined treatments to treat mental illness must be interconnected with their parts, work in harmony, and work together to be effective. The success of any mental illness treatment will depend on a combination of alternative combined treatments, and a combined treatment alone may not eliminate or reduce significantly the mental illness symptoms.

- Which combined treatments have you been using?

- Choose one combined treatment below that you have been using.

    1. Developing new concepts
    2. Making new friends
    3. Developing new expectations
    4. Learning about my disease
    5. Learning from my past
    6. Changing my lifestyle
    7. Attending church
    8. Developing discipline
    9. Focusing on my spirituality
    10. Developing new behaviors
    11. Developing new coping skills
    12. Complying with my medication
    13. Developing responsibilities
    14. Learning how to cope with feelings
    15. Participating in pleasurable activities
    16. Attending AA/NA meetings
    17. Developing new ways of thinking
    18. Other _____

 ✧ What is this combined treatment about?

 ✧ How have you been using this combined treatment?

Topic 2: Increasing Insight of Unconscious Mechanisms

Exercise 1: Defense Mechanisms

Purpose:

    A. To increase insight of unconscious pathological defense mechanisms.
    B. To discuss different kinds of defense mechanisms.

Hints and Procedures:

Distribute the handouts provided below, and use the four questions to start the group discussion related to the defense mechanisms. Encourage the group discussion by using the defense mechanisms from the list. Encourage the members to come up with examples of each defense mechanism discussed.

Group Session Model:

The group session was developed in order to discuss different kinds of defense mechanisms, as they can have a direct or indirect impact on the mental illness treatment process. The clinician started the group session by reviewing the general principles of defense mechanisms including the definition, reasons to use them, and their negative consequences. Then the members were given handouts containing a list of the most common defense mechanisms. The group discussion focused on the dynamic of the psychological conflicts hidden by the defense mechanisms followed by specific examples.

The patient reported to the session with a high level of anxiety as he was irritated and easily agitated. As the session progressed, the patient demonstrated a varied level of interest by asking relevant questions related to the topic discussed. He maintained direct eye contact and required moderate encouragement to engage in the group discussion. Upon approach, the patient stated, "I was in denial of my drug addiction for a long time. I did not accept the fact that I was addicted."

The group discussed unconscious defense mechanisms that hindered or prevented improvements of the members' conditions. The patient received support from the group on his admission of his denial as a defense mechanism blocking his recovery. The patient appeared able to grasp the concepts and information discussed during the group discussion.

The future group sessions will continue to assist the patient in reducing the use of defense mechanisms blocking his treatment process.

Topic 2: Increasing Insight of Unconscious Mechanisms

Exercise 1: Defense Mechanisms

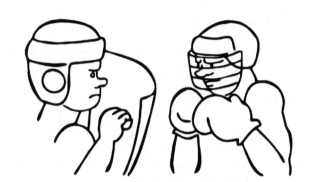

What is a defense mechanism?

Today, the group insight session will be all about defense mechanisms. However, be careful! Defense mechanisms in psychology are not what we commonly know. In psychology, they have different meanings. Do you know the difference?

- Choose one of the questions below for which you think you know the answer.

    A. What is the definition of a defense mechanism?[1]
    B. Why do we use defense mechanisms?[1]
    C. Are defense mechanisms positive or negative? Why?[2]
    D. Are defense mechanisms conscious or unconscious? Are people aware of them?[3]

- Choose one of the defense mechanisms below that you would like to discuss with your peers. Follow the two first examples and provide your own.

    1. Minimizing: "It is not so bad; I am only having three drinks."
    2. Rationalizing: "I had a hard day. Anyone who has had a hard day needs to relax."
    3. Denying: _____
    4. Lying: _____
    5. Monopolizing: _____
    6. Manipulating: _____
    7. Justifying: _____
    8. Procrastinating: _____
    9. Escaping: _____
    10. Compensating: _____
    11. Sublimating: _____
    12. Resisting: _____
    13. Excusing: _____
    14. Blaming: _____

---

[1] Pathological defense mechanisms are psychological strategies used by individuals to hide or to distort reality.

[2] They are negative and lead to maladaptive behaviors that will eventually affect the mental health of the individual.

[3] They are unconscious, and people are unaware of them.

Topic 2: Increasing Insight of Unconscious Mechanisms

Exercise 2: Defense Mechanism Resistance

Purpose:

    A. To increase insight into areas of resistance.
    B. To eliminate blocks to a successful treatment.

Hints and Procedures:

Review the concepts of defense mechanisms including the pathological definition, reasons to use them, and their consequences. Distribute the handouts provided below, and promote the group discussion about the members' areas of resistance, including alternative combined psychotherapies to break the cycle of resistance.

Group Session Model:

The group session was developed in order to help the members increase insight into areas of resistance blocking the success of their treatments. In order to facilitate the group discussion, the members were given handouts containing a list of possible areas of resistance and were asked to identify which areas they have been resisting. The group discussion focused on exploring alternative combined psychotherapies to break the cycle of resistance.

In the session, the patient was isolated, guarded, and sad. He was observed squinting his eyes and sitting upright. The patient was able to participate in the group activity only upon being prompted and encouraged by the clinician. The patient commented, "I have actively resisted complying with my medications. Sometimes when I feel good, I think that I do not need to take my medications anymore."

The members discussed the patient's situation, and provided him with training in some ways to remove stumbling blocks or cope with his resistance to ensure his treatment progress and stabilization. He responded positively to the training received.

The staff has recommended that the patient continue attending this level of service to gain new insight into other areas of resistance blocking the success of his treatment.

Topic 2: Increasing Insight of Unconscious Mechanisms

Exercise 2: Defense Mechanism Resistance

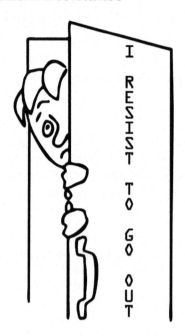

Resistance is a common defense mechanism among human beings. During the course of your treatment, you may face resistance in some areas, which would block your progress. So, it is important to identify which areas you have been resisting.

- I believe I have resisted ...

    ☐ 1. accepting that I am mentally ill and I need treatment.
    ☐ 2. accepting that I did something wrong and I need help.
    ☐ 3. participating in activities.
    ☐ 4. participating in the group discussion.
    ☐ 5. talking about myself.
    ☐ 6. socializing.
    ☐ 7. complying with my medications.
    ☐ 8. developing and implementing goals.
    ☐ 9. making any changes to improve myself.
    ☐ 10. Other _____

    ✧ How can you break the cycle of resistance above?

Topic 2: Increasing Insight of Unconscious Mechanisms

Exercise 3: Defense Mechanism Excuses

Purpose:

    A. To gain insight into defense mechanism excuses.
    B. To discuss the use of excuses in the treatment process.

Hints and Procedures:

Distribute the handouts provided below, and read the information related to the defensive mechanism excuses. Review the definition of a defense mechanism. Encourage the members to identify their excuses in their treatment processes and focus the group discussion on how to break the cycle of excuses impeding their treatment progress.

Group Session Model:

This group session was designed to assist the members in gaining insight into defense mechanism excuses and the negative impact on their treatments. The clinician initiated the group discussion by reviewing with the members the definition of a defense mechanism. Then the members were asked to use handouts containing information, questions, and a list of several defensive mechanism excuses. The members were encouraged to identify their defense mechanism excuses and how to break the cycle of the excuses impeding their treatment progress.

The patient had a dominant depressive mental status consistent with his increased level of sadness. He remained withdrawn and apprehensive, and sat distant from the members. The patient was receptive to moderate prompting, and on approach, the patient stated, "I think one of my excuses for not doing much except watching television is related to the fact that I am mentally ill. Now, I understand that in order to improve myself, I need to learn how to stop using my mental illness as an excuse."

The patient's opinion was supported by the members. The patient demonstrated an understanding of several other defense mechanism excuses discussed during the group discussion.

Continued group psychotherapy is recommended for this patient to monitor his progress toward reducing the use of defense mechanisms in order to decrease his mental illness symptoms and stabilize his mood.

Topic 2: Increasing Insight of Unconscious Mechanisms

Exercise 3: Defense Mechanism Excuses

Making excuses is a very common defense mechanism, which may impede your treatment progress. Basically, there are four kinds of excuses: realistic, justifiable, unrealistic, and unjustifiable. All them can lead to negative consequences. Being able to recognize the constant use of excuses should be the first step toward making changes for the success of your treatment.

- **Please answer questions A–D below:**

    A. Which one of the excuses below have you used?

    1. Avoiding unpleasant things
    2. Not assuming responsibility
    3. Justifying action
    4. Justifying behavior
    5. Avoiding unpleasant feelings
    6. Not blaming oneself
    7. Justifying attitude
    8. Hiding the reality

    B. Can you identify one realistic and justifiable excuse below?

    C. Can you identify at least two unrealistic and unjustifiable excuses below?

    1. I have no motivation.
    2. I have no money.
    3. I have no place to go.
    4. I have no friends.
    5. I am mentally ill.
    6. I have no transportation.
    7. I have a bad alarm clock.
    8. I have no family support.
    9. I always have bad traffic.
    10. I am too old for that.
    11. I always forget.
    12. I have no job.
    13. I have family problems.
    14. I live too far away.
    15. I am too tired.

    D. Which behaviors below may apply to the excuses on the questions above?

    1. Missing the group sessions
    2. Coming late to the group sessions
    3. Not complying with treatment
    4. Refusing to be active
    5. Difficulty staying in the group sessions
    6. Not complying with my medication
    7. Not participating in the group discussion
    8. Other _____

Topic 2: Increasing Insight of Unconscious Mechanisms

Exercise 4: Defense Mechanism Blaming and Criticizing

Purpose:

    A. To stop blaming and criticizing.
    B. To discuss negative consequences of defense mechanism blaming and criticizing.
    C. To discuss pros and cons of criticizing.

Hints and Procedures:

While the handouts are being distributed, introduce the topic by reviewing with the members the concepts of pathological defense mechanisms including the definition and examples. Use the questions and information from the handouts to promote the group discussion about defense mechanism blaming and criticizing.

Group Session Model:

The group session was focused on helping the members to stop blaming and criticizing as defense pathological mechanisms. To facilitate the group discussion, the members were given handouts containing questions and information related to defense mechanism blaming and criticizing.

The patient had a sad facial expression and rigid posture, and was detached, suggesting a dominant depressive mental status. The patient was receptive to moderate prompting and was able to participate in the group discussion with minimal guidance. The patient chose one of the questions to discuss and commented, "I think I have been blaming and criticizing my family too much, because they have not provided me with an outstanding education."

The members concurred with the patient about his defense mechanism blaming. The patient reviewed his understanding of the concepts discussed and agreed to stop blaming and criticizing others in order to make progress.

The future sessions will continue to help the patient break the cycle of the pathological defense mechanisms as part of the process to help him reach mood stabilization.

Topic 2: Increasing Insight of Unconscious Mechanisms

Exercise 4: Defense Mechanism Blaming and Criticizing

Blaming and criticizing are typical defense mechanisms considered to be unhappy parts of the human experience. Criticism is often unproductive in eliciting any positive changes. Generally, people are not aware when they are using defense mechanisms, they are not aware of the negative consequences they might have in life, and this may have been affecting your stabilization process as well.

- Choose one question below to discuss with your peers.

    A. Why do people blame others?
    B. Why do people negatively criticize?
    C. What can be the negative consequences of blaming and criticizing?
    D. How can you tell whether a criticism is valuable or useless?
    E. Whom have you been blaming or criticizing? Why?

- Which defense mechanisms below are blaming (B) or criticizing (C)?

    ( ) 1. "You are always doing that! Stop!" ( ) 7. "You are always saying that. Why?"
    ( ) 2. "You never do that to please me."   ( ) 8. "You are constantly on top of me."
    ( ) 3. "You should have told me sooner."   ( ) 9. "Everyone in my family treats me badly."
    ( ) 4. "It is how I was raised."   ( ) 10. "It is because this happened to me."
    ( ) 5. "You wanted me to do that."   ( ) 11. "You get in the way of everything I do."
    ( ) 6. "The food here is always bad."   ( ) 12. "This group psychotherapy is very boring."

    ✧ Have you ever used any of the defense mechanisms above? Which ones?

    ✧ How can we break the cycle of defense mechanisms?

Topic 3: Improving Happiness

Exercise 1: Concepts of Happiness

Purpose:

A. To discuss concepts and ideas about happiness.

Hints and Procedures:

Distribute the handouts provided below. Introduce the topic by reading the caption: "Happy or not happy? It is better to be happy!" Use the brainstorming techniques to encourage the members to answer the questions related to happiness. Go around and ask the members for their own definitions of happiness. Continue the group discussion with the remaining questions.

Group Session Model:

The group session activity consisted of discussing concepts and ideas about happiness. In order to facilitate the group discussion, the members were provided with handouts containing several questions related to happiness. The clinician encouraged the members to express their opinions about happiness including its definition, concepts, thoughts, philosophy, and meanings.

The patient's mood and affect was depressed and best described by his sad facial expression, lack of motivation, isolation, and disengagement. In response to the topic discussed, the patient stated, "For me, at the present, happiness means stabilization. When I am stable, I feel happy."

The patient's idea of happiness was supported by the members. The group discussion continued exploring the secret of happiness, where happiness comes from, and the key for happiness among others. The patient was receptive to the feedback. Also, he appeared to grasp much of the information discussed in order to work on his own happiness improvement.

The staff will continue to stimulate the patient's interest in the topics being discussed in the group sessions in order to facilitate his stabilization process.

Topic 3: Improving Happiness

Exercise 1: Concepts of Happiness

Happy or not happy?

It is better to be happy!

Regardless of your idea or concept of happiness, we are all human beings, looking for happiness in a direct or indirect way. Therefore, are you "happy or not happy? It is better to be happy!" However, happiness may not happen automatically; you must look for it.

- How can we look for happiness? The answers to the questions below may help you to find out.[1]

    1. What is happiness?
    2. Does happiness exist? Why?
    3. What is the secret of happiness?
    4. Does money bring happiness?
    5. Will you be happy if you can find what happiness consists of? Why?
    6. Does happiness come from inside or outside oneself?
    7. May action bring happiness?
    8. Could there be happiness without action?
    9. Is success the key for happiness, or is happiness the key for success?
    10. What are the grand essentials of happiness?

---

[1] Suggested answers:
  1. Happiness is an inner state of well-being and contentment.
  2. For some people, happiness may not exist, but people can have at least moments of happiness in life.
  3. The secret of happiness is our willingness to choose life.
  4. Happiness may not really be in possessing money; it lies in the joy of achievement and in the thrill of a creative effort.
  5. You will never live if you are looking for the meaning of life.
  6. Happiness must come from within.
  7–8. Action may not always bring happiness, but there is no happiness without action.
  9. Happiness is the key for success. If you love what you are doing, you will be successful.
  10. The grand essentials of happiness are something to do, something to love, and something to hope for.

Topic 3: Improving Happiness

Exercise 2: Searching for Happiness

Purpose:

    A. To identify areas to work on to improve happiness.
    B. To encourage action in searching for happiness.

Hints and Procedures:

Warm up the group discussion with this caption: "Action may not always bring happiness, but there is no happiness without action." Use the handouts provided below to facilitate the group discussion. Ask the members to identify their "waiting list areas" for happiness. List and discuss these waiting list areas in the group. Promote the group discussion about actions the members should take to improve their happiness through each waiting list area.

Group Session Model:

The focus of this group session was to identify areas to work on to improve happiness. The clinician warmed up the group discussion with this caption: "Action may not always bring happiness, but there is no happiness without action." Then the members were asked to use handouts containing questions and a guide to search for happiness. The members were encouraged to identify their "waiting list areas" for happiness. The group discussion focused on actions to be taken to improve happiness through the identified areas.

In prior sessions, the patient came in depressed. Similarly, in this session, the patient was observed as being isolated from his peers, and having a sad facial expression, downcast eyes, and limited interaction. In a weak voice, the patient explained to the group, "One of my waiting list areas is my release from the mandatory treatment by the court. There is not too much that I can do now for my happiness besides coming here every day and trying to improve myself as much as possible."

The members provided the patient with encouragement concerning his action taken, which later on may contribute to his happiness improvement. The patient responded positively to the encouragement.

The future sessions will continue to provide the patient with constructive advice and encourage him to share his feelings in group sessions. He will be encouraged to make the necessary commitments and take actions that can lead to improved happiness in his life.

Topic 3: Improving Happiness

Exercise 2: Searching for Happiness

Go for happiness or wait to be happy?

"Action may not always bring happiness, but there is no happiness without action." So, what must we do?

- Should we go for happiness or wait to be happy?

    ✧ Do you ever find yourself ...

    ☐ 1. waiting for a better life?
    ☐ 2. waiting for a stabilization?
    ☐ 3. waiting for fewer worries in life?
    ☐ 4. waiting to finish this program?
    ☐ 5. waiting to meet a court-mandated treatment program requirement?
    ☐ 6. waiting to get a job?
    ☐ 7. waiting for magic to happen?
    ☐ 8. waiting for a better relationship?
    ☐ 9. waiting for a better place to live?
    ☐ 10. Other _____

    ✧ Which action should you take for each waiting list above?

    For waiting list number ( ) I need to _____
    For waiting list number ( ) I need to _____
    For waiting list number ( ) I need to _____

Topic 3: Improving Happiness

Exercise 3: Recipe for Happiness

Purpose:

    A. To develop a "recipe" for happiness.
    B. To share constructive advice to improve happiness.

Hints and Procedures:

Distribute the handouts provided below, and start the group discussion by asking the members the first and second questions related to happiness. Encourage the members to use the appropriate "ingredients" and develop a fun "recipe for happiness." Encourage the group discussion on how to use the ingredients for happiness.

Group Session Model:

The group session consisted of training the members in the use of the exercise developing a "recipe" for happiness. The members were given handouts containing questions related to happiness and a list of possible "ingredients" to develop a "recipe for happiness." The members were encouraged to choose the ingredients from the list and develop their own recipes for happiness. The group discussion focused on how to use the ingredients to develop the recipe for happiness.

The patient has regularly manifested symptoms suggesting depression. He was observed as being sad, and having poor eye contact, a lack of motivation, and a low energy level. In response to the topic discussed, the patient made the following comment: "In my opinion, I believe that love should be the most important ingredient for any happiness recipe." The patient continued his idea by saying, "I must learn to love myself first if I want to be happy."

The patient's opinion and comment were supported by the members. The patient was receptive to the support. Also, he enthusiastically suggested adding many other valuable ingredients to develop his own recipe for happiness.

The future sessions will continue to assist and encourage the patient's understanding of the components to improve his happiness and stabilize his mood.

Topic 3: Improving Happiness

Exercise 3: Recipe for Happiness

Regardless of your concept or idea of happiness, everyone can benefit from a little more happiness.

- But, the point is this:
  - ✧ What makes people happy?
  - ✧ What should be the recipe for happiness?

- Choose at least one ingredient below to add to your recipe for happiness.

    1. Loving myself
    2. Having more freedom
    3. Improving my hope
    4. Focusing on my potential
    5. Focusing on my spirituality
    6. Loving others
    7. Developing goals (specify)
    8. Increasing my social support system
    9. Developing discipline
    10. Improving my functional level
    11. Focusing on my abilities
    12. Increasing my level of self-esteem
    13. Increasing my participation in activities
    14. Other _____

  ✧ How can you use the ingredient you chose above?

Topic 3: Improving Happiness

Exercise 4: Free Elements

Purpose:

    A. To explore free elements in life to improve happiness.
    B. To develop appreciation for the environment.
    C. To raise insight about opportunities for enjoyment that are free.

Hints and Procedures:

Distribute the handouts provided below, and encourage the members to complete the word find activity related to free elements in life. While the handouts are been distributed, provide the members with some examples of enjoyable things in life that are free. They may include some of the following physical elements: beach, ocean, sky, moon, and sunset. Behavioral elements may include love, a warm greeting, and a smile. Encourage the members to identify activities associated with the free elements in life that they would like to become involved in (e.g., meditating under the moon).

Group Session Model:

The purpose of this group session was to raise the members' insight about opportunities for enjoyment in life that do not cost money. The members were encouraged to complete a word find exercise containing physical and behavioral elements in life that are free. Then they were encouraged to identity activities associated with the elements. Examples of free physical and behavioral elements were provided by the clinician at the beginning of the session.

The patient's mood and affect was depressed with symptoms similar to the previous sessions. He was observed to have downcast eyes and tense posture, and to be isolated. On approach and upon being prompted by the clinician, the patient stated, "Well, speech is free, and I can use speech to talk to people and make new friends."

The patient's idea was supported by the members and made part of the group discussion. Other examples of free physical and behavioral elements were suggested by the members. The patient was open to the group discussion and appreciated ideas about mood-enhancing elements that are free. Among them, the members discussed friendly greetings, smiling, and a hopeful attitude.

The staff will continue to stimulate the patient's appreciation for free elements in life to improve his happiness, help him decrease mental illness symptoms, and improve his level of functioning.

Topic 3: Improving Happiness

Exercise 4: Free Elements

Being in contact with nature is psychologically healthy and may be a very enjoyable activity. Just listening to the sound of birds singing or watching the little baby ducks following their mother may be a very exciting spectacle. The good thing is that there are many elements in life that are free, and all them may help bring you happiness.

- Please answer the following questions:

  ◆ How many free elements in life can you identify in the word find below?[1]

U	R	A	I	N	S	C	O	M	P	R	E	H	E	N	S	I	O	N	U
C	O	M	P	A	S	S	I	O	N	I	M	O	U	N	T	A	I	N	A
S	S	O	E	I	T	N	T	L	O	V	E	K	I	N	D	N	E	S	S
U	K	O	A	R	A	O	F	O	R	E	S	T	S	M	I	L	E	B	C
N	Y	N	C	Y	R	W	A	T	E	R	R	E	S	P	E	C	T	I	P
A	F	F	E	C	T	I	O	N	F	R	I	E	N	D	B	E	A	C	H

  ◆ Why do you think these elements above are free?

  ◆ Can you identify at least two activities to do with these elements above?

---

[1] Key words: affection, air, beach, compassion, comprehension, forest, friend, kindness, love, moon, mountain, peace, rain, respect, river, sky, smile, snow, star, sun, water.

Topic 3: Improving Happiness

Exercise 5: Opportunities for Enjoyment

Purpose:

    A. To explore community resources and opportunities for enjoyment.
    B. To explore leisure activities.

Hints and Procedures:

While the handouts are being passed out, warm up the group discussion by asking the members about what makes them happy. Ask the members to identify activities that make them happy. Encourage the members to think about available resources and opportunities for enjoyment in the community. Challenge each member to make a commitment to become involved in at least one leisure activity in the community. Assist the members to overcome obstacles before beginning any activity.

Group Session Model:

The subject of the group session was to explore leisure activities and resources available in the community. The members were provided with a word find exercise with several activities and questions related to opportunities for enjoyment. Each member was challenged to choose and become engaged in at least one leisure activity.

As in prior sessions, the patient came to the group with a depressive mental status congruent with his affect. He was initially isolated from the others, had a sad facial expression, and was tired. The patient was able to participate but required some direction and encouragement. Upon prompting, the patient chose one leisure activity and commented, "Reading is one activity that I used to do before, and I really used to enjoy doing that."

The therapeutic intervention consisted of stimulating and assisting the patients to explore strategies to implement the activities discussed. For instance, it was suggested that the patient start visiting the public library where he could find some interesting books and become involved in reading. The patient was receptive to the suggestion and agreed to explore the idea in the future.

The future sessions will continue to encourage the patient's involvement in leisure activities as an outlet to improve his happiness and stabilize his mood.

Topic 3: Improving Happiness

Exercise 5: Opportunities for Enjoyment

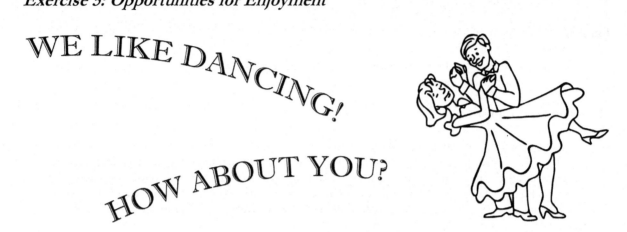

WE LIKE DANCING! HOW ABOUT YOU?

Involvement in leisure activities should be part of our entire lives. The benefits of leisure activities are numerous. They can lead to friendship, relaxation, fun, and self-improvement. All of these together may bring us happiness. So, what can make you happy?

- Please complete the tasks below:

  ◆ Identify at least two activities in the word find below that can make you happy.[1]

G	B	O	W	L	I	N	G	S	O	C	I	A	L	I	Z	I	N	G	B
A	C	D	R	R	S	W	I	M	M	I	N	G	O	P	S	D	P	V	I
R	A	A	I	E	A	C	R	U	I	S	I	N	G	A	I	R	R	I	C
D	M	N	T	A	I	P	A	I	N	T	I	N	G	I	N	A	A	S	Y
E	P	C	I	D	L	F	I	S	H	I	N	G	I	N	G	W	Y	I	C
N	I	I	N	I	I	S	A	I	L	I	N	G	A	R	I	I	I	T	L
I	N	N	G	N	N	S	U	R	U	N	N	I	N	G	N	N	N	I	I
N	G	G	O	G	G	M	E	D	I	T	A	T	I	N	G	G	G	N	N
G	O	L	F	I	N	G	S	I	G	H	T	S	E	E	I	N	G	G	G

  ◆ Where in the community can you become involved in these activities?

  ◆ What do you need to do to become involved in these activities?

---

[1] Key words: bicycling, bowling, camping, cruising, dancing, drawing, fishing, gardening, golfing, meditating, painting, praying, reading, running, sailing, sightseeing, singing, socializing, swimming, visiting, writing.

Topic 4: Understanding Oneself

Exercise 1: "Who Am I?"

Purpose:

    A. To get a sense of oneself.
    B. To establish a sense of oneself.
    C. To increase a sense of oneself.

Hints and Procedures:

Initiate the group discussion by encouraging the members to answer the following question: *"Who am I?"* Provide the members with the handouts. Encourage the members to answer the remaining questions and complete the statements related to the sense of oneself. Remind the members that we get a sense of ourselves from praise and criticism, but it is the praise that builds a healthy sense of oneself.

Group Session Model:

The group session was designed to assist the members in getting a sense of themselves. The members were encouraged to use handouts containing questions and statements to be completed related to the sense of oneself. The group activity started with a brief review about concepts of a sense of oneself, including its definition and how we get it.

The patient was observed to be depressed as evidenced by his sadness, low energy level, isolation, and lack of motivation. The patient was able to identify one fact describing him as part of the exercise to help get a sense of oneself. He added, "One fact that can describe me is that I came from a multicultural background, and this makes me feel unique."

The members empathized with the patient's uniqueness as an important element defining him. The patient was receptive to the feedback and agreed to use the exercise in the future to continue increasing his sense of self.

The professional team has determined that the patient will continue to need this level of service in order to increase his sense of self, decrease his depressive symptoms, and prevent psychiatric hospitalization.

Topic 4: Understanding Oneself

Exercise 1: "Who Am I?"

You should use your sense of self as the reference point to determine who you are and what you want to do with your life. So, knowing about yourself is very important to help you establish your sense of self.

- But ...

    A. what is a healthy sense of oneself?
    B. where do we get it from?
    C. how can we build it?
    D. how can we lose it?

- Do you know who you are?

- Please complete the following statements about yourself:

    1. I am _____
    2. I am competent in _____
    3. I am able to _____
    4. I should discard the following from myself: _____
    5. I should continue _____
    6. One of my positive values is _____
    7. One of my weaknesses is _____
    8. One fact that can describe me is _____
    9. The meaning of life for me is _____
    10. I will _____

Topic 4: Understanding Oneself

Exercise 2: Perception of Oneself

Purpose:

    A. To understand personal uniqueness.

Hints and Procedures:

Distribute the handouts provided below, and read the text on personal uniqueness. Start the group session by asking the members for the meaning of uniqueness. Encourage each member to complete the "I statements" and discuss at least one personal unique quality that they like most about themselves.

Group Session Model:

The group activity consisted of helping the members understand their personal uniqueness. At the beginning of the session, the members were asked for the meaning of uniqueness. Then they were provided with handouts with questions and "I statements" to be completed regarding their personal uniqueness. Each member was encouraged to discuss at least one personal unique quality that he or she likes most about him or herself.

The patient came to the session depressed as evidenced by his downcast eyes, sad facial expression, and guarded and non-spontaneous behaviors. As the session progressed and upon moderate prompting, the patient became involved in the group discussion. The patient used an "I statement" and stated, "I think I have been saved by God from the world of addiction, and this accomplishment is now part of my uniqueness."

The members empathized with the patient's uniqueness. The patient was receptive to the group empathy and was supportive of the other members' uniqueness.

The staff will continue to assist and encourage the patient to keep track of personal uniqueness in order to better understand himself.

Topic 4: Understanding Oneself

Exercise 2: Perception of Oneself

Although we can share many similarities with each other, nobody in this world is exactly like you—you are unique. You need to keep track of your uniqueness in the formation of your ideas, when trying to understand yourself, and in the relationships you have with others.

- Answering the questions and completing the "I statements" below will help you understand more about your uniqueness.

  ◆ What is the meaning of uniqueness?[1]

  ◆ What is your uniqueness?

1. I am _____	6. I know _____
2. I want _____	7. I should _____
3. I have _____	8. I feel _____
4. I can _____	9. I wish _____
5. I think _____	10. I plan _____

  ◆ Which personal unique quality above do you like most about yourself? Why?

---

[1] One's uniqueness can mean kinds of differences when compared to someone else.

Topic 4: Understanding Oneself

Exercise 3: "What Is Going Wrong with Me?"

Purpose:

    A. To gain insight into personal problems.

Hints and Procedures:

While the handouts are being distributed, warm up the group discussion with this caption: "What is going wrong with me?" Encourage the members to use the self-questioning technique as a way of gaining insight into their personal problems. If somebody is in denial, the focus should be on reasons to be in the program—i.e., chronic and enduring mental illnesses, court-mandated treatment orders, previous psychiatric hospitalizations, and addiction problems.

Group Session Model:

The focus of this group session was on helping the members gain insight into personal problems. The clinician introduced the topic by reviewing with the members the use of the self-questioning technique. Handouts were distributed to the members with questions including the caption "What is going wrong with me?" to help them identify and address current personal problems.

The patient appeared hyper-verbal, spoke in an agitated manner, and was fidgeting constantly. The patient answered one of the questions with the following comment: "I lost my marriage because I was not able to understand what was important in life. I was working too much, and when I had my first nervous breakdown about one year ago, my wife divorced me. So, at the present, I am very depressed and grieving the loss of my wife."

The clinician assisted the patient in understanding the root causes of his feelings, highlighting the importance of maintaining a healthier perspective and positive attitude as part of the grief process. The patient was able to challenge his current negative feelings associated with his current depressive episode.

The staff will continue to encourage the patient to participate actively in the group sessions as part of the process to overcome his depressive symptoms.

Topic 4: Understanding Oneself

Exercise 3: "What Is Going Wrong with Me?"

What is going wrong with me?

Being mentally ill can bring many problems in a person's life. Many things can go wrong, and one of the first steps in the recovery process is to understand what is going wrong with you. You should be able to identify and recognize your own problems. It requires insight through the use of a self-questioning technique.

- Practice the self-questioning technique by using the following questions:

    1. What is going wrong with me?

    2. If nothing is wrong, why am I in this group?

    3. What is one of my biggest problems?

    4. What have I been doing to solve it?

    5. If I cannot solve it, what should I do?

Topic 4: Understanding Oneself

Exercise 4: "Life Is ..."

Purpose:

    A. To increase perception of life.

Hints and Procedures:

Use the handouts provided below, and encourage the members to come up with their own perceptions of life by completing this phrase: "Life for me is ... because ..." Discuss the importance of letting go of the past and focusing on the present. Encourage the members to develop a positive outlook concerning their present lives and their futures. Discuss the philosophy of life and provide examples of life's positive perceptions.

Group Session Model:

The clinician initiated the group session by reviewing with the members the philosophy of life and providing several examples of life's positive perceptions. The members were asked to use handouts with a list of several ideas of life's perceptions. Then the members were encouraged to come up with their own perceptions of life by completing the phrase "Life for me is ... because ..." and explaining the reasons for their life perceptions.

As in the prior sessions, the patient had good hygiene, fair eye contact, but a sad facial expression, and he required prompting to participate in the group activity and discussion. On approach, he commented, "Life for me is like a trial, because I have been learning the good and the bad things."

The members empathized with the patient's perception of life. The clinician suggested to the patient to focus on life's positive outlook and positive perspectives toward the future. Also, the members discussed the importance of letting go of the past and focusing on the present. The patient was receptive to the therapeutic intervention and the members' comments.

The staff will continue to assist the patient with further therapeutic interventions aimed at developing a positive perception of life to support his mental health and his mood stabilization.

Topic 4: Understanding Oneself

Exercise 4: "Life Is ..."

Life is like being born again!

Our current perceptions of life are probably the fruits of our pasts and will also be parts of our futures. If our pasts were good, we may have positive reflections of life in the present. But, if they were bad, we may have negative philosophies of life in the present. In this case, it is important to let go of the past and focus on the here and now.

- What is life for you?

  Life for me is ...

  1. boring.
  2. like a carnival.
  3. like waves in the sea.
  4. relaxing.
  5. okay when stable.
  6. hopeless.
  7. difficult.
  8. a challenge.
  9. a transition.
  10. like a game of cards.
  11. like a tango.
  12. having energy.
  13. miserable.
  14. spiritual growth.
  15. new opportunities to learn.
  16. new reflections of living.
  17. a new way of behaving.
  18. full of new adventures.
  19. good only with money.
  20. nice with friends.
  21. a trial of good and bad.
  22. _____

  ✧ Why is life like that for you?

  ✧ Is that important or not important for you? Why?

Topic 4: Understanding Oneself

Exercise 5: "Looking Back or Looking Ahead?"

Purpose:

    A. To promote intrapersonal awareness.
    B. To better understand oneself.

Hints and Procedures:

Present to the members this concept: "You cannot go ahead in life by always looking back." Distribute the handouts provided below, and encourage the members to answer the questions related to the above concept.

Group Session Model:

The group session was designed to help the members promote intrapersonal awareness. The clinician presented as a topic for discussion this concept: "You cannot go ahead in life by always looking back." Then the members were provided with handouts containing questions related to the above concept. The members were challenged to look ahead instead of looking back.

The patient has regularly displayed symptoms suggesting depression as evidenced by his isolated behavior, downcast eyes, and limited self-disclosure. However, the patient was receptive to moderate prompting. He came up with one of his feelings and behaviors related to the above concept by stating, "Sometimes, I feel frustrated because I cannot motivate myself to look for work. I guess that is because I got fired from my last job."

The clinician prompted the group discussion about the importance of letting go of the past and focusing on the present. The patient seemed to have gained insight about the idea of focusing on the present instead of the past.

The professional team will continue to provide the patient with new opportunities to better understand him in supporting his stabilization process.

208 ■ *Group Insight*

Topic 4: Understanding Oneself

Exercise 5: "Looking Back or Looking Ahead?"

"You cannot go ahead in life by always looking back."

Many concepts in life can help promote intrapersonal awareness, which can lead to a better understanding of oneself. Some people get stuck in the past and cannot move on.

- Please answer the following questions:

    1. Can we forget the past?
    2. Can we get anything from the past? If yes, what?
    3. How can we look ahead?
    4. How can we neutralize the past?
    5. How can we forgive?
    6. Are you stuck in your past? Why?
    7. What can the concept above tell you about yourself?
    8. Is there anything from your past impeding your present progress? What?

Topic 4: Understanding Oneself

Exercise 6: "Getting to Know You"

Purpose:

    A. To increase knowledge about each group member.
    B. To encourage group sharing.

Hints and Procedures:

Make a copy of the attached handout and prepare the material for the group task. Discuss with the members the importance of increasing knowledge about each member in order to increase one's understanding of oneself.

Group Session Model:

The group session focused on helping the members to increase knowledge about each other through the use of the exercise called "Getting to Know You." In order to facilitate the group process and discussion, the members were provided with small pieces of paper containing statements with personal information to be completed. Each member was asked to randomly pick up one statement from a small box, read it aloud, and complete it.

Although the patient was observed with good hygiene and fair grooming, his demeanor in this session was similar to the prior sessions, with a low energy level, lack of motivation, and difficulty concentrating. The patient expressed his thoughts on the topic, stating, "In my spare time, I would like to spend more time with kids. I love kids, and I think I have something special that makes me attracted to them as well."

The members encouraged the patient to explore activities in the community, such as volunteer work where he can spend time with kids. The patient agreed to pursue the idea as well as was motivated to use the "Getting to Know You" exercise in the future in order to continue learning more about him.

The staff has recommended that the patient continue treatment to reduce his symptoms of mental illness to a more manageable level. The professional team will facilitate this process to assist the patient to meet this goal.

Topic 4: Understanding Oneself

Exercise 6: "Getting to Know You"

- **Instructions to the Group Leader**

   Cut out the statements below. Fold each statement and put it in a container or small box. Arrange the members in a circle. Pass the box around the room and ask each member to pick up one statement and read it aloud. Some members may need the statement read to them. Be sure everyone in the group listens to the statements. Encourage group sharing. After the person has completed the statement, ask others in the group if they would like to complete the same statement, too. Variation: play music while the container is being passed. When the music stops, the person holding the box takes a statement and completes it.

1. If I won a million dollars, I would …	11. In my spare time, I would like to …
2. I do … to make me feel happy.	12. I plan to … when leaving this program.
3. My favorite pet is …	13. A memory of a happy time in my life is …
4. My advice to my peers here is …	14. My favorite color is … The color I dislike is …
5. My favorite time of the year is … because …	15. My favorite TV program is …
6. My goals for the future are …	16. One of my best qualities is …
7. One of my weaknesses is …	17. One of my special talents is …
8. One thing I am proud of is …	18. The most important thing in my life is …
9. The best trip I ever took was …	19. Today I would like to have … for dinner.
10. The name of my children or siblings are …	20. My favorite former job is …

Topic 4: Understanding Oneself

Exercise 7: My Personal Story

Purpose:

    A. To share personal real life stories.
    B. To increase understanding of oneself.

Hints and Procedures:

Review with the members the benefits of sharing personal, real-life stories (e.g., it may be fun, interesting, a good learning experience, and help to increase understanding of oneself). Provide the members with the handouts. Encourage each member to tell a true, significant, fun, and humorous life story. Review the benefits of the activity with the members.

Group Session Model:

The focus of this group session was aimed at increasing understanding of oneself by sharing personal life stories. The clinician introduced the topic by explaining to the members that everyone has a significant, fun, humorous, and true story in life. The members were invited to share their personal life stories, make brief narratives of them, and say what they have to do with their lives.

The patient came to the session well groomed and appropriately dressed. However, his dominant mood remained depressed and consistent with his sad affect, detachment, and lack of motivation. The patient stated, "I remember when my first son said Dad to me. He was about two years old. It was a happy moment that I will always cherish."

The members empathized with the patient's experience. During the course of the group discussion, the patient became aware that sharing and listening to each other's life stories may offer interesting and fun experiences, as well as helping increase understanding of oneself.

The staff recommended the patient's continuous attendance at this level of service in order to self-disclose other personal information to increase his understanding of himself and reach his mood stabilization.

Topic 4: Understanding Oneself

Exercise 7: My Personal Story

Sharing personal life stories may offer an interesting and fun experience. Also, it can help us understand more about each other. Practically, everybody has a personal story in life that may have been a very significant and learning experience.

- Think about a significant, fun, humorous, and true story in your life.

    ✧ Make a brief narrative of your personal story:

    _____
    _____
    _____
    _____

    ✧ What has such a story to do with you?

    _____

PART VIII

GROUP MEDICATION

TOPICS 1–4

WITH

FOURTEEN EXERCISES

Topic 1: Discussing Principles of Psychotropic Medications

Exercise 1: Medication and Symptoms

Purpose:

    A. To increase knowledge about depressive symptoms and medications.

Hints and Procedures:

Use the handouts provided below, and encourage the members to review their major depressive symptoms. Make a list of the depressive symptoms on the blackboard. Use the questions to promote a group discussion about common antidepressant psychotropic medications used to treat depressive symptoms. Ask the members to name their own psychotropic medications and the purpose of them (e.g., improving mood, improving sleep, and decreasing anxiety).

Group Session Model:

The purpose of this group session was to increase the members' knowledge about major depressive symptoms and the corresponding psychotropic medications. The nurse started the group discussion by reviewing with the members the importance of educating oneself about the antidepressant psychotropic medications used to treat depressive symptoms. In order to facilitate the group discussion, the members were provided with handouts with questions related to the subject discussed.

The patient came to the session with a dominant depressed mood and affect as evidenced by his poor eye contact, initial isolated behavior, and tearful and sad facial expression. When encouraged by the nurse to share information regarding his medication, the patient added, "I suffer from major depression, and one of my symptoms is insomnia." The patient continued with his ideas by saying, "I am taking Reactivan to help me sleep better, and this has been helping me."

The nurse and the members reinforced the patient's compliance with the prescribed medicine to treat his symptoms. The patient was receptive to the reinforcement.

The medical team will continue to provide the patient with the medication management aimed at educating the patient on the use and compliance of psychotropic medications as part of his treatment process.

Topic 1: Discussing Principles of Psychotropic Medications

Exercise 1: Medication and Symptoms

Increasing knowledge about the symptoms of your mental illness and the corresponding psychotropic medications should be a very important step for the success of your treatment. You can accomplish that with education, supportive interaction, and appropriate choices. Let's start educating ourselves today about a very common mental illness called major depressive disorder and its corresponding medications.

- Please answer the following questions:

    1. What are the most common symptoms of major depressive disorder?
    2. Which antidepressant psychotropic medications are used to treat this mental illness?
    3. Are you currently taking any antidepressant psychotropic medications? Which ones?
    4. If not, which kind of psychotropic medications are you currently taking?
    5. Do you know for which symptoms you are taking these medications?
    6. Can you stop taking antidepressant psychotropic medications if you feel good? Why?
    7. Can major depressive disorder be cured with psychotropic medications?
    8. What else do you know about symptoms and medications?

Topic 1: Discussing Principles of Psychotropic Medications

Exercise 2: Medication Supply

Purpose:

    A. To keep medication supply current.
    B. To discuss responsibilities related to medication supply.

Hints and Procedures:

Warm up the group discussion with this expression: "To refill or to run out? That is the question!" Distribute the handouts provided below, and encourage the members to answer the true-or-false statements to express their opinions about refilling, running out, and responsibilities related to their medication supplies. Use the content of each statement to promote the group discussion related to the medication supply.

Group Session Model:

The purpose of this group session was to discuss responsibilities related to medication supply. The nurse warmed up the group discussion with this expression: "To refill or to run out? That is the question!" Then the members were provided with handouts with true-or-false statements related to medication supply. The group discussion focused on the content of each statement related to the medication supply.

During the session, the patient had a dominant depressive mental status consistent with his sad affect, rigid posture, and quiet and isolated behaviors. The patient was receptive to moderate prompting and expressed himself by stating, "I understand that refilling my medication on time is my responsibility, and I never should run out of my medication if I want to continue being stable."

The nurse and the members concurred with the patient's opinion, to which he was receptive. Also, the patient was receptive to many other pieces of pertinent information supporting his responsibility for his medication supply.

The medical team has determined that the patient will continue to require attendance at this group medication session in order to empower himself to take responsibility for his medication supply.

Topic 1: Discussing Principles of Psychotropic Medications

Exercise 2: Medication Supply

Keeping your medication supply current should be one of your responsibilities for the success of your treatment. Running out of your medication may have adverse negative consequences on your treatment process. But the point is this: how can you be sure that you will never run out of your medication?

- In the parenthesis below, mark (T) for true or (F) for false for the following statements:[1]

  ( ) 1. Refilling my medication on time is my responsibility.
  ( ) 2. If I run out of my medication, I should borrow some from my peers.
  ( ) 3. If I run out of my medication, I should immediately contact the nurse or the psychiatrist.
  ( ) 4. Using a pillbox can help me keep track of my medication supply.
  ( ) 5. It is okay to go a couple of days without medication until I get my refill.
  ( ) 6. It might be a good idea to skip some doses to avoid running out.
  ( ) 7. My medication supply should be current only while coming to this program.
  ( ) 8. I should prioritize attending this group session first and my medication supply second.
  ( ) 9. Running out of my medication supply can lead to a relapse of my psychiatric symptoms.
  ( ) 10. Medication supply is a fact and not a myth.

- ✧ Discuss your answers with your nurse. Have fun!

---

[1] Answer key: 1) True, 2) False, 3) True, 4) True, 5) False, 6) False, 7) False, 8) False, 9) True, 10) True.

Topic 1: Discussing Principles of Psychotropic Medications

Exercise 3: Medication Safety

Purpose:

    A. To understand medication safety.
    B. To discuss steps to keep medications safe.

Hints and Procedures:

Discuss the implication of medication safety for the success of treatment. Use the handouts provided below, and encourage the members to complete the word find exercise related to medication safety. Promote the group discussion with each step to keep medications safe.

Group Session Model:

The focus of the group session was to discuss steps to keep medications safe. The nurse emphasized the implication of medication safety for the success of the treatment. The members were given handouts with a word find exercise related to medication safety, and the group discussion focused on each step to be taken to keep medications safe.

The patient appeared quiet, sad, tired, isolated, and guarded, suggesting a dominant depressive mood. The nurse asked if the patient was taking the medications regularly, and he replied, "I take my medications on time, and whenever I have any question about my medication, I talk to the nurse or with my psychiatrist."

The patient's comments made part of the group discussion focus on supporting many other steps to keep medications safe.

The future group sessions will continue to educate the patient about his medication management and his medication compliance.

Topic 1: Discussing Principles of Psychotropic Medications

Exercise 3: Medication Safety

Keeping your medications safe should be an integral part of your treatment process, especially when you start taking a new medication. There are many steps you should take to make sure you are keeping your medications safe. What are these steps?

- Try to find the steps for medications safe in the word find and statements below.[1]

P	M	E	D	I	C	A	T	I	O	N	U	R	S	E	L	A	B	E	L
R	E	A	D	T	I	M	E	P	S	Y	C	H	I	A	T	R	I	S	T
I	N	F	O	R	M	A	T	I	O	N	S	E	P	A	R	A	T	E	O
A	D	O	C	T	O	R	P	I	L	L	B	O	X	H	A	N	D	L	E
B	R	I	G	H	T	A	R	E	A	S	A	F	E	T	Y	A	R	E	S

1. It's important that you ----------- the label of your medication.
2. If you have any questions or concerns about your --------------------, you should ask the ----------- or the ---------------.
3. You should take your medications in a -----------.
4. You should read the ---------------- for any information about your medications.
5. Medications taken by other family members should be kept ----------------------.
6. Medications should be kept in their original containers except when using a -------------.
7. You should read any ----------- provided by the pharmacist.
8. You must take your medication as prescribed by the -------------.
9. You must take your medication on -----------.
10. The success of your treatment depends on how you ------------- your medication.

---

[1] Answer key: 1. read; 2. medication, psychiatrist, nurse; 3. bright area; 4. label; 5. separate; 6. pill box; 7. information; 8. doctor; 9. time; 10. handle.

Topic 2: Increasing Knowledge of Psychotropic Medications

Exercise 1: Medication Action

Purpose:

    A. To increase knowledge about medication action.

Hints and Procedures:

    Provide the members with the handouts. Promote the group discussion about the different groups of psychotropic medications. They may include antipsychotic, antidepressant, anti-anxiety, antimanic, and stimulant medications.

Group Session Model:

    This group session was developed in order to increase the members' knowledge about their medications action. The nurse introduced the topic by discussing with the members the importance of learning everything about their medications. Then the members were provided with handouts with true-or-false statements related to different groups of psychotropic medications. The group discussion focused on the content of each statement.

    During the session, the patient presented to the group as depressed. The patient was disheveled, had marginal hygiene, and was withdrawn. He was able to participate only upon being prompted and encouraged. The patient stated, "I suffer from major depression. I have learned from my psychiatrist that the antidepressant medication I have been taking helps stabilize the chemicals in my brain."

    The nurse confirmed this information. The nurse explained to the group that neurotransmitters are chemical components needed for normal brain functions. The benefit of antidepressant drugs is reducing depressive symptoms, such as sadness, hopelessness, and lack of interest. The patient was receptive to the new information received.

    The group medication sessions will continue in order to increase the patient's knowledge of psychotropic medications and monitor his compliance.

Topic 2: Increasing Knowledge of Psychotropic Medications

Exercise 1: Medication Action

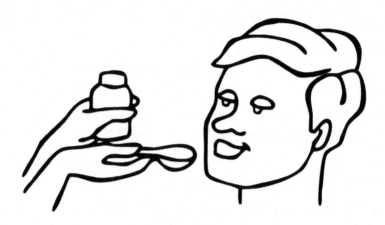

You should learn everything about your medications. It is important for you to be well informed about the psychiatric medications you have been taking, such as dose, purpose, and actions. So, let's check today how much you know about this subject.

- Are the statements below true (T) or false (F)?[1]

    1. Neurotransmitters are chemical components needed for normal brain functions. ( )
    2. Psychotropic medications cure mental illness. ( )
    3. Psychotropic medications lessen mental illness. ( )
    4. Stimulant medications can turn off the voices heard by some people. ( )
    5. Antidepressant medications can lift the dark, heavy moods of depression. ( )
    6. Chlorpromazine is a kind of anti-anxiety medication. ( )
    7. Antipsychotic medications are used to treat people with schizophrenia. ( )
    8. Antimanic medications are used to reduce sadness and hopelessness. ( )
    9. Anti-anxiety medications can help improve one's sleeping pattern. ( )
    10. People can perceive reality more accurately with stimulant medications. ( )

 ✧ Why do you think your answers above are true or false?

---

[1] Answer key: 1) True, 2) False, 3) True, 4) False, 5) True, 6) False, 7) True, 8) False, 9) True, 10) False.

Topic 2: Increasing Knowledge of Psychotropic Medications

Exercise 2: Medication Benefits

Purpose:

    A. To discuss the benefits of psychotherapeutic medications.

Hints and Procedures:

Review the concept "the success of treatment would depend on a combination of multiple treatments," meaning medication and psychotherapy. Distribute the handouts provided below, and assist the members in answering the true-or-false statements regarding the psychotherapeutic medications. Promote the group discussion with the information of each statement. Focus the group discussion on the benefits of medication.

Group Session Model:

The focus of this group session was on psychotherapeutic medication benefits. The nurse warmed up the group discussion by reviewing the concept "the success of treatment would depend on a combination of multiple treatments," including medication and psychotherapy. Then the members were given handouts with true-or-false statements related to psychotherapeutic medication benefits. The members were encouraged to use the content of each statement to promote the group discussion on the benefits of medication.

The patient was observed to be excessively depressed and sad, as evidenced by his constricted mood, isolated behavior, and tearful facial expression. The patient required prompting and encouragement from the nurse in order to participate in the group discussion. The patient stated, "I have already learned that psychotherapeutic medications cannot cure my bipolar disorder, but they can help me to get myself stable."

The nurse concurred with the patient's assessment of medication. During the course of the session, the patient had an opportunity to discuss with the nurse many other psychotherapeutic medication benefits, including relieving psychosis and anxiety, preventing relapse, and improving mood and affect. The patient was receptive to the group discussion.

The medical team will continue to encourage the patient's adherence to his medication regimen as part of his stabilization process.

Topic 2: Increasing Knowledge of Psychotropic Medications

Exercise 2: Medication Benefits

Psychotherapeutic medications are an increasingly important element for the successful treatment of mental illness. For many patients, a combination of psychotherapy and medications can be an effective method of treatment.

- **Are the statements below true (T) or false (F)?**[1]

    Psychotherapeutic medications ...

    ( ) 1. must be part of the treatment of any mental illness.
    ( ) 2. make people fall in love with each other.
    ( ) 3. can help improve one's level of functioning.
    ( ) 4. relieve psychotic symptoms but not depression.
    ( ) 5. can help improve one's mood and affect.
    ( ) 6. relieve anxiety but increase panic attacks.
    ( ) 7. relieve obsessive-compulsive disorder symptoms.
    ( ) 8. can cure addiction to drugs and alcohol.
    ( ) 9. stimulate people who are too depressed to start talking and respond better.
    ( ) 10. decrease anxiety and decrease the need to sleep.

    ✧ **Discuss your responses with the nurse.**

---

[1] Answer key: 1) True, 2) False, 3) True, 4) False, 5) True, 6) False, 7) True, 8) False, 9) True, 10) False.

Topic 2: Increasing Knowledge of Psychotropic Medications

Exercise 3: Medication Side Effects

Purpose:

A. To discuss the most common side effects of psychotropic medications.

Hints and Procedures:

Use the handouts provided below, and encourage each member to identify at least one medication side effect. Discuss with the members ways to deal with the side effects produced by the medications.

Group Session Model:

This group session was about medication side effects. In order to facilitate the group activity and discussion, the members were provided with handouts with a list of the most common medication side effects. Each member was encouraged to identify at least one medication side effect to discuss with the group. The group discussion focused on exploring ways to control the medication side effects.

In the session, the patient was disheveled, withdrawn, somewhat guarded, and anxious at times. The patient required moderate prompting to participate in the group discussion. In response to the medication side effects discussed, the patient stated, "I have been gaining some weight after I started taking my antipsychotic medications, but now I have been doing some exercises to help me control my weight."

The nurse encouraged the patient to continue taking his antipsychotic medications despite its side effects, as well as to continue doing physical exercise to control his weight. The patient was receptive to the encouragement.

The medical team will continue to provide the patient with the opportunities to learn other important information about psychotropic medications in order to reinforce his compliance.

Topic 2: Increasing Knowledge of Psychotropic Medications

Exercise 3: Medication Side Effects

What is this medication doing to my tongue?

Most side effects of antipsychotic medications are mild. Many common side effects lessen or disappear after the first few weeks of treatment.

- Please answer the following questions:

    ❖ What medication side effects below apply to you?

☐ 1. Dry mouth	☐ 7. Constipation	☐ 13. Weight gain
☐ 2. Dizziness	☐ 8. Drowsiness	☐ 14. Increased heart rate
☐ 3. Fatigue	☐ 9. Sexual problems	☐ 15. Blurred vision
☐ 4. Skin rashes	☐ 10. Sunburn	☐ 16. Bladder problems
☐ 5. Nausea	☐ 11. Anxiety	☐ 17. Confusion
☐ 6. Weakness	☐ 12. Menstrual problems	☐ 18. Other _____

    ❖ What can you do with these side effects?[1]

---

[1] Dry mouth: drink water and chew sugarless gum. Constipation: eat bran cereals, prunes, fruit, and vegetables. Weight gain: do exercise. Dizziness: rising from the bed or chair slowly is helpful. Drowsiness: sedating antidepressants should be taken at bedtime to minimize daytime drowsiness. Also, ask your doctor to prescribe a different medication; changing the dosage or schedule, or prescribing an additional medication can help control side effects.

Topic 2: Increasing Knowledge of Psychotropic Medications

Exercise 4: Medication Abuse

Purpose:

A. To increase knowledge about medication abuse.

Hints and Procedures:

Encourage the members to talk about medication abuse. Review the danger associated with mixing depressants like barbiturates, benzodiazepines, and stimulants. Provide the members with the handouts. Encourage and assist the members to complete the statements with the keywords related to medication abuse. Promote the group discussion with the content of each statement. Clarify information, and educate the members about risks, including permanent injury and death associated with the misuse of any medication.

Group Session Model:

During this group medication session, the nurse encouraged the members to talk about medication abuse. The nurse started the group discussion by reviewing with the members some of the dangers associated with mixing depressants with stimulants. Then the members were provided with handouts containing statements to be completed about medication abuse. The group discussion focused on the content of each statement related to the negative consequences of the misuse of medication.

The patient has regularly showed a moderate level of depression as evidenced by a tendency to be slightly isolated and somewhat guarded, and to have a sad facial expression; he also seemed tired. As the session progressed and upon being prompted, the patient became interactive, was able to complete one of the keywords exercises, and made a valuable comment related to that statement. He stated, "Prescription medications are powerful substances. I know this is true because one of my best friends died of an overdose of a stimulant."

The nurse praised the patient for his participation and for the valuable comment, to which he was receptive.

Continued group medication management sessions are still necessary for this patient as part of the treatment process to help him reach mood stabilization.

Topic 2: Increasing Knowledge of Psychotropic Medications

Exercise 4: Medication Abuse

Pharmaceuticals taken without a prescription or outside a doctor's supervision can be just as dangerous as taking illicit drugs or abusing alcohol.

- Please fill in the blanks with the correct words below:[1]

   1. Medication abuse is the _____ or overuse of any medication or drug, including alcohol.
   2. Prescription medications are _____ substances.
   3. Prescription medications, like all drugs, can cause _____ interactions with other drugs or chemicals in the body.
   4. Many street drugs have no _____ benefits.
   5. The risk for _____ exists when drugs are used in ways other than as prescribed.
   6. _____ medications can be abused by people who take more than the recommended dose.
   7. Many pills look pretty much the same, but depending on the drug and the dosage, the effects can vary greatly from mild to _____.
   8. Depressant medications should never be combined with any medication or substance that causes drowsiness, including _____ pain medicines.
   9. If depressant medications are combined with other medications or drugs, they can slow down breathing, or slow both the heart and respiration, which can be _____.
   10. Stimulants should never be mixed with _____.

---

[1] Keywords: 1. misuse, 2. powerful, 3. dangerous, 4. therapeutic, 5. addiction, 6. prescription, 7. lethal, 8. legitimate, 9. fatal, 10. antidepressant.

Topic 2: Increasing Knowledge of Psychotropic Medications

Exercise 5: Medication and Nutrition

Purpose:

    A. To increase knowledge about medication and nutrition.
    B. To develop an ideal diet for proper digestion, absorption, and assimilation.

Hints and Procedures:

Make a single copy from the attached handout. Then cover the keywords on the bottom, make several copies, and distribute them to the members. Encourage and assist the members to find out the missing words for the incomplete statements. Promote the group discussion by exploring the content of each statement.

Group Session Model:

The subject of this group session was medication regimens and proper nutrition to protect the digestive system. The members were given handouts with several incomplete statements about medication and nutrition. They were asked to complete the statements with the missing words. The group discussion focused on the content of each statement with an emphasis on the ideal diet for proper digestion, absorption, and assimilation.

The patient appeared depressed as evidenced by his low energy level, sadness, and isolation. Also, he was observed to have a tearful facial expression and had limited interaction. In response to the topic discussed, the patient commented, "Since I started taking psychotropic medications, I drink a lot of water every day as I was instructed, and this has helped me to absorb my medication."

The nurse supported the patient's following instructions. The group continued to discuss other important ingredients for an ideal diet, such as decreasing food portions, decreasing salt intake, drinking fruit juice daily, and eating fruits and vegetables. The patient agreed to add these ingredients to his own diet on a daily basis.

The medical team will continue to encourage the patient to comply with his current medication regimen, including the ideal diet items discussed during the group session.

Topic 2: Increasing Knowledge of Psychotropic Medications

Exercise 5: Medication and Nutrition

How am I nutritionally?

The answer to the question above is important for all, but may be especially critical for persons with mental health problems. Why? The brain is a chemical factory that produces different brain chemicals through the use of nutrients. If the brain receives improper amounts of nutrient building blocks, we can expect health problems.

- Please fill in the statements below with the appropriate words.[1]

  1. The most important chemicals produced by the brain are _____, _____, and _____ .
  2. Nutrients, such as _____ _____, _____, and _____ are _____ materials the brain needs for _____ .
  3. Enzymes speed up _____ reactions and play a vital role in _____ .
  4. Physiological and physical _____ of nutrition and exercise include desired _____ maintenance, improved _____ glucose levels, and _____ blood pressure.
  5. Medication _____ may be reduced with appropriate nutrition and _____ .
  6. _____ food portions, _____ salt intake, and drinking plenty of _____ daily should be part of an ideal diet for proper _____ .
  7. The ideal diet for proper digestion, _____, and assimilation include _____ juice, _____, and vegetables.

  ✦ Discuss with your nurse at least one of your answers above.

---

[1] Keywords: 1. norepinephrine, serotonin, dopamine; 2. amino acids, vitamins and minerals, raw, syntheses; 3. chemical, mental health; 4. benefits, weight, blood, lowered; 5. doses, exercise; 6. decreasing, lowing, water, digestion; 7. absorption, grape, fruits.

Topic 2: Increasing Knowledge of Psychotropic Medications

Exercise 6: Stopping Medication

Purpose:

    A. To discuss the negative consequences of choosing to stop taking medication.
    B. To discuss the role of medication in preventing relapse.

Hints and Procedures:

While the handouts are being distributed, start brainstorming with members with this question: "What if I stop taking my medication?" Challenge each member to identify at least one dangerous effect or negative consequence of choosing to stop taking his or her medications.

Group Session Model:

The group session was about the dangerous effects and the negative consequences of choosing to stop taking medication. The nurse focused the group discussion on the role of medication in preventing relapse. Handouts with information about choosing to stop taking medication were provided to the members to facilitate the group discussion. Each member was challenged to identify at least one dangerous effect or negative consequence related to choosing to stop taking their medication.

At the beginning of the session, the patient's initial mood was depressed and consistent with his sad facial expression and isolation. As the session progressed, the patient was noted to be anxious as evidenced by a tense posture, difficulty concentrating, and excessive talking. In response to the topic of stopping medication, the patient commented, "I relapsed before because I stopped taking my medication. I was feeling good, and I thought that I no longer had to take any medication."

Comments by the nurse further reinforced the importance of continuing to take his medication, to which he was in agreement.

The medical team has determined that the patient will need to continue attending the group medication sessions in order to acquire new knowledge of psychotropic medication and monitor his compliance.

230 ■ *Group Medication*

Topic 2: Increasing Knowledge of Psychotropic Medications

Exercise 6: Stopping Medication

What if a stop taking my medication?

Choosing to stop taking your medication is, of course, your choice. However, some medications may cause extremely unpleasant and possibly dangerous effects in your life when you stop taking them abruptly. So, what would these dangerous effects or negative consequences be?[1]

- **If I stop taking my medication, the consequences may be the following:**

    Consequence 1:
    _____

    Consequence 2:
    _____

    Consequence 3:
    _____

    Consequence 4:
    _____

    Consequence 5:
    _____

---

[1] The most critical should be relapsing. Relapsing may include negative consequences such as legal problems, loss of freedom, jail, decompensation of psychiatric symptoms, suicide, and hospitalization.

Topic 3: Discussing Psychotropic Medications Compliance

Exercise 1: Medication Strategies

Purpose:

    A. To learn ways of remembering to take medications.
    B. To explore strategies to manage medications.

Hints and Procedures:

Review some implications or negative consequences of not taking medications as prescribed. Focus the group discussion on the importance of a medication routine. Distribute the handouts provided below, and assist the members in completing the statements related to the medication strategies. Challenge each member to identify and discuss at least one strategy to remember to take his or her medications. If he or she has already been using any of them, ask how they have been working for him or her and process their reliability. Use the content of each statement to promote the group discussion related to the medication strategies.

Group Session Model:

The purpose of this group session was to learn ways of remembering to take medications. At the beginning of the session, the nurse reviewed some implications or negative consequences of not taking medications as prescribed. Handouts with statements to be completed related to strategies to remember to take medications were distributed. The members were asked to identify which strategies would work for them. The group discussion focused on the content of each statement related to the medication strategies.

The patient appeared fidgeting, had an anxious affect, and talked in a loud tone of voice. The patient stated, "Although I live in an adult living facility, I have to be responsible to take my medications on time. So, I use an alarm clock to remind me of the time I should take my medications."

Positive feedback was provided by the nurse regarding the patient's medication strategy. The patient responded positively to the feedback. Also, he recognized that medication routines are critical in maintaining his mental health and his functional level.

The medical professionals have suggested the patient's continuous attendance to the group medication sessions in order to acquire new information related to medication issues supporting his stabilization and to prevent him from relapsing from his mental illness.

Topic 3: Discussing Psychotropic Medications Compliance

Exercise 1: Medication Strategies

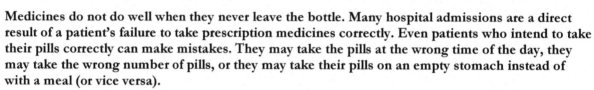

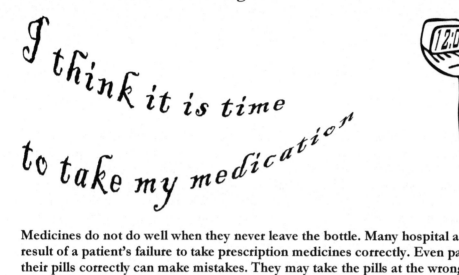

Medicines do not do well when they never leave the bottle. Many hospital admissions are a direct result of a patient's failure to take prescription medicines correctly. Even patients who intend to take their pills correctly can make mistakes. They may take the pills at the wrong time of the day, they may take the wrong number of pills, or they may take their pills on an empty stomach instead of with a meal (or vice versa).

- Which strategy can you use to manage your medication well?

- Match the first column with the words from the second column.[1]

I can take my medication …

( ) 1. at _____	a) weekly schedule
( ) 2. by putting them in a _____	b) note
( ) 3. by using a _____	c) activity
( ) 4. by having _____ to remind me_____	d) bedtime
( ) 5. by leaving it in a _____ place_____	e) somebody
( ) 6. by leaving myself a _____ to remind me_____	f) home
( ) 7. by organizing a _____ _____	g) pillbox
( ) 8. with an_____ that I do everyday_____	h) timer
( ) 9. with _____	i) teeth
( ) 10. with me when leaving _____	j) meals
( ) 11. when I brush my _____	k) visible
( ) 12. _____	l) _____

✧ Which strategy above would work for you? Why do you think so?

---

[1] Answer key: 1) d, 2) g, 3) h, 4) e, 5) k, 6) b, 7) a, 8) c, 9) j, 10) f, 11) i.

Topic 3: Discussing Psychotropic Medications Compliance

Exercise 2: Medication Tracking

Purpose:

    A. To learn how to keep track of medications.
    B. To discuss the importance of a medication list.

Hints and Procedures:

While the handouts are being passed out, start the group session by reviewing with the members the importance of keeping a medication list. Encourage each member to express his or her opinions about the topic discussed. Promote the group discussion with the content of each statement related to medication tracking.

Group Session Model:

The focus of the group session was to learn how to keep track of medications. The members were provided with handouts with true-or-false statements regarding medication tracking. The nurse started the group session by reviewing with the members the importance of keeping a medication list. The group discussion focused on the content of each statement related to medication tracking.

In prior sessions, the patient came in depressed. Similarly, in this session, the patient was observed to be quiet, withdrawn, and somewhat distracted; to have a sad facial expression; and to be guarded at times. Upon moderate prompting, the patient noted, "I keep good track of my medications because I had a problem before. I ran out of pills. So, now, I always keep my medication list updated."

The nurse provided the patient with reinforcement and encouragement to continue keeping good track of his medications through the use of his medication list. The patient was receptive to the support received.

The medical team will continue to provide the patient with opportunities to learn new information and concepts related to medication compliance as part of the process to help the patient reach mood stabilization.

Topic 3: Discussing Psychotropic Medications Compliance

Exercise 2: Medication Tracking

A complete list of all your medications is very important for proper medical care. Keeping track of your medications should be a very important strategy to help you comply with your medications. One way of doing that is to make a list of all your medications.

- What is a medication list?

- Are the statements below true (T) or false (F)?[1]

A medication list …	T or F?
1. can prevent medication errors if it is accessible.	( )
2. should not be accessible to physicians.	( )
3. should include all medications prescribed or not prescribed by a physician.	( )
4. should be accessible to any lawyer that needs to know about your case.	( )
5. can help physicians provide higher quality care.	( )
6. does not need to be updated since it is done.	( )
7. can provide medication information in case of an emergency.	( )
8. should include vitamins, minerals, and herbs, but not over-the-counter medications.	( )
9. can make the physician's job much easier.	( )
10. can help psychotherapists provide individual psychotherapy sessions.	( )
11. can provide accurate medication information of interactions between other drugs.	( )
12. should be kept in a safe locker where nobody can have access.	( )

    ◆ Choose one of the statements above to discuss with your nurse.

---

[1] Answer key: 1) True, 2) False, 3) True, 4) False, 5) True, 6) False, 7) True, 8) False, 9) True, 10) False, 11) True, 12) False.

Topic 3: Discussing Psychotropic Medications Compliance

Exercise 3: Medication Compliance and Noncompliance

Purpose:

    A. To discuss reasons for noncompliance with medication.
    B. To understand the importance of medication compliance.

Hints and Procedures:

Distribute the handouts provided below. Start the group discussion with the meaning of medication compliance. Discuss the different meanings of medication noncompliance. Continue the group discussion by discussing reasons why people do not take their medications. Challenge each member to come up with solutions for how to break the cycle of resistance to medication compliance.

Group Session Model:

This group session discussed reasons for noncompliance of medication plans. The nurse introduced the topic by reviewing with the members the meaning of medication compliance. Then the members were provided with handouts with different meanings of medication noncompliance and a list of reasons why people do not take their medication. The group discussion focused on the content of each statement and solutions to break the cycle of resistance to medication compliance.

The patient manifested symptoms suggesting a dominant depressive mental status. Among them, the patient was observed to be sad and isolated, to have poor eye contact, and to have a low level of motivation. When prompted by the nurse to share with the members one of his reasons for not taking his medication, the patient stated, "I was not taking my medication because the pills made me sick. Now, I know that it is important for me to take my medications every day because I do not want to go to the hospital again."

The nurse encouraged the patient to comply with his medication and explained that side effects are common. The patient was receptive to the nurse's encouragement.

The medical team will continue to educate the patient about medication management as well as enforce his compliance with his medication.

Topic 3: Discussing Psychotropic Medications Compliance

Exercise 3: Medication Compliance and Noncompliance

To comply or not to comply? That is the question!

People do not take their medications for many reasons. One of the first and the most important steps toward the success of your treatment is to educate yourself about what the medication is and why it is important to take it. Medication compliance means taking medications as prescribed. But, noncompliance with the medications may have many different meanings.

- Put a checkmark next to the correct definitions of medication noncompliance below:[1]

    (a) taking the wrong dose
    (b) skipping doses
    (c) taking incorrect medication
    (d) taking medication at the wrong time
    (e) not filling a prescription
    (f) stopping medication before its course is completed

    ☐ only "a" is correct
    ☐ only "a," "b," and "c" are correct
    ☐ all statements are correct
    ☐ only "a," "c," and "f" are correct
    ☐ only "e" and "f" are correct
    ☐ only "b" is correct

- What can be done for somebody not taking medications because of the following reasons?

    1. Forgetting to take them
    2. Forgetting to refill them
    3. Believing the drugs are not effective
    4. Believing that there is no need to take them
    5. Having no symptoms or having the symptoms go away
    6. Having discomfort or frightening side effects
    7. Having difficulty getting the prescription filled
    8. Having difficulty opening the bottle or swallowing the drug
    9. Having an unpleasant taste or smell
    10. Feeling confused by all the drugs that have to be taken
    11. Being prevented from doing other things when taking the medication
    12. Wanting to save money

---

[1] All statements are correct.

Topic 4: Discussing Medications and Other Drugs

Exercise 1: Alcohol Abuse

Purpose:

    A. To identify physiological and psychological symptoms of alcohol abuse.
    B. To discuss the negative effects of alcohol abuse on the body's system.

Hints and Procedures:

Review the disease concept as related to alcohol abuse. Use the handouts provided below to facilitate the group discussion about several negative physiological and psychological consequences of alcohol abuse. Discuss how symptoms develop and their impact on all life dimensions (e.g., physiological, mental, emotional, and social).

Group Session Model:

The group session focused on identifying physiological and psychological symptoms of alcohol abuse. The nurse initiated the group discussion by reviewing with the members the disease concept as related to alcohol abuse. To facilitate the group discussion, the members were given handouts with a word find exercise to be completed related to alcohol abuse symptoms.

The patient appeared fidgety, guarded, and isolated, had an initial anxious facial expression, and spoke in a hesitant manner. The patient shared with the members his previous experience with alcohol by stating, "In my teenager years, I used to drink a lot, and I had to be hospitalized because of a mild pancreas inflammation. Now, I never drink, and I have been sober for years."

The patient was praised for his participation and for sharing his past negative experience with his alcohol abuse. During the course of the group discussion, the patient reviewed his understanding of the many other negative physiological and psychological effects of alcohol abuse.

The group medication sessions will continue to educate the patient on medication management and the negative impact of other drugs on the body's system.

Topic 4: Discussing Medications and Other Drugs

Exercise 1: Alcohol Abuse

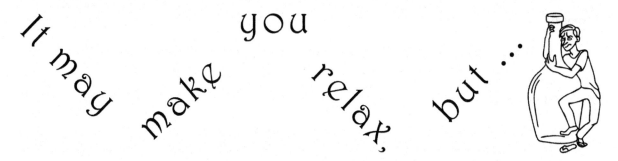

Alcoholism is a disease in which the consumption of alcohol or the need for alcohol becomes an addiction. This can cause emotional, mental, physical, and social harm to the alcoholic, and his or her friends or family. It can lead to many physiological complications affecting several body systems. So, let's test your knowledge today.

- What symptoms of alcohol intoxication can you identify in the crossword below?[1]

C	O	G	N	I	T	I	V	E	I	M	P	A	I	R	M	E	N	T	A
C	O	O	R	D	I	N	A	T	I	O	N	P	R	O	B	L	E	M	S
O	I	N	A	T	T	E	N	T	I	O	N	S	T	A	N	D	I	N	G
M	E	B	E	H	A	V	I	O	R	A	L	P	R	O	B	L	E	M	S
P	R	O	B	L	E	M	S	M	E	M	O	R	Y	S	E	X	U	A	L
S	L	U	R	R	E	D	D	R	O	W	S	I	N	N	E	S	S	T	E
S	P	E	E	C	H	A	G	G	R	E	S	S	I	O	N	C	O	M	A

- Are the statements below true (T) or false (F)?[2]

    ( ) 1. Alcohol abuse can affect the gastrointestinal tract, leading to ulcers and peripheral edema.
    ( ) 2. Short-term effects of alcoholism may include hallucinations and tremors only.
    ( ) 3. Withdrawal symptoms may include seizures, hallucinations, and tremors.
    ( ) 4. Long-term effects of alcoholism may include pancreas inflammation and insomnia.
    ( ) 5. Long-term effects of alcoholism may include liver complications, depression, and anxiety.
    ( ) 6. Long-term effects of alcoholism may include sexual dysfunction and nerve improvement.
    ( ) 7. Long-term effects of alcoholism include only heart disease and nutrition complications.
    ( ) 8. Death is not a typical consequence of prolonged alcoholism.

---

[1] Keywords: aggression, behavioral problems, cognitive impairment, coma, coordination problems, drowsiness, inattention, memory problems, sexual problems, slurred speech, standing problems.

[2] Answer key: 1) True, 2) False, 3) True, 4) True, 5) True, 6) False, 7) False, 8) False.

Topic 4: Discussing Medications and Other Drugs

Exercise 2: Caffeine Effects

Purpose:

      A. To learn reasons why caffeine should be avoided.
      B. To discuss the negative physiological and psychological effects of caffeine.

Hints and Procedures:

Distribute the handouts provided below. Warm up the group discussion by using the caption: "Would coffee do anything good to your health?" Promote the group discussion by answering and discussing the content of each question related to the effects of caffeine.

Group Session Model:

The focus of this group session was on discussing the negative physiological and psychological effects of caffeine. The nurse warmed up the group discussion by asking the members the question, "Would coffee do anything good to your health?" Then the members were given handouts with questions related to caffeine consumption, and the group discussion focused on the content of each question. The nurse assisted the members in answering the questions by adding extra information to them.

The patient reported to the session with a depressed mood, best described by his sadness, isolation tendency, and lack of motivation. The patient commented on the negative effects of caffeine on his body as follows: "As for me, I cannot drink coffee because it makes me anxious and nervous."

The patient was praised for his participation. He was receptive to the praised received. Also, during the course of the group discussion, the patient became aware of many other negative effects of caffeine on the body as discussed by the members.

The medical team will continue to educate the patient on drugs and medication management as part of the patient's treatment process to reach his mood stabilization.

Topic 4: Discussing Medications and Other Drugs

Exercise 2: Caffeine Effects

Would coffee do anything good to your health?

There are many reasons why you should avoid caffeine. It can have many negative effects on your body, and it can affect you mentally and psychologically as well. So, let's try to discuss some of the most harmful effects of this so common drug that most people take every day.

- **Questions for group discussion:**[1]

    1. What is caffeine?
    2. Where can we find caffeine?
    3. How long does it take to feel caffeine's effects?
    4. What are the most common negative effects of caffeine?
    5. What are the short-term effects of caffeine on the body?
    6. What are the symptoms of caffeine overdose?
    7. How does caffeine affect sleep?
    8. Can caffeine lead to addiction and withdrawal?
    9. What are the withdrawal symptoms of caffeine?
    10. How can we cut down on caffeine?

---

[1] Answer key:
1. Caffeine is a stimulant.
2. It can be found in many foods, drinks, and medicines.
3. It takes about fifteen to forty-five minutes to reach peak levels.
4. Caffeine produces insomnia, increases anxiety and nervousness, increases jaw tension, and raises blood pressure and heart palpitations.
5. It increases heartbeat, respiration, basal metabolic rate, gastro-enteric reflexes, and the production of stomach acid and urine.
6. Overdose can lead to restlessness, dizziness, nausea, headaches, tense muscles, delirium, diarrhea, vomiting, and convulsions.
7. It can cause restlessness and difficulty falling asleep.
8. Caffeine is addictive and causes withdrawal symptoms after cessation of heavy use.
9. They may include craving, confusion, tiredness, lethargy, and headaches.
10. Caffeine should be cut down gradually.

Summary

Group Psychotherapy: Exercises at Hand takes a very practical approach to each topic and corresponding exercises for group psychotherapy sessions. A key goal of the book series is to gradually derive meaningful applications to group therapy in order to provide clinicians with an interesting, useful, and stimulating experience.

Dealing constructively with any unfinished business related to mental problems has a profound impact. We, the clinicians, open the doors to help others make real changes in their lives. Our vision of what is possible is expanded from the traditional old-fashioned ineffective ways to provide psychological services to more effective and practical ways of treating mentally ill patients. When we are able to do something constructive, we move closer to the mental illness healing process.

I have taken my second big step in providing topics and exercises for group self-esteem, depression, behavior, goals, insight, and medication in this second volume of *Group Psychotherapy: Exercises at Hand*. These exercises can be an effective means of intervening in mental health problems and an important tool in the clinician's repertoire of group psychotherapy materials. This group therapy program is an especially attractive option, because the material is specific for these six types of groups: self-esteem, depression, behavior, goals, insight, and medication. The topics and exercises are well organized, practical, easy to use, and can be used in both outpatient and inpatient settings. However, the effectiveness of treatment provided by group psychotherapy sessions would be greatly increased if this book were used with other topics and exercises on conducting mental health care groups. In the therapeutic intervention, a clinician should not use only one or two types of group therapy but several different groups of treatments with an abundance of topics and exercises, such as those presented in this volume, in volume 1, and in volume 3 of *Group Psychotherapy: Exercises at Hand*.

References

Corey, G. (1985). *Theory and Practice of Group Counseling* (2nd Ed.). Belmont, CA: Brooks/Cole.

Davis, M., Eshelman, E. R., & Mckay, M. (1995). *The Relaxation & Stress Reduction Workbook* (4th Ed.). Oakland, CA: New Harbinger.

Dossick, J., & Shea, E. (1988). *Creative Therapy: 52 Exercises for Groups.* Sarasota, FL: Professional Resource Exchange.

Dossick, J., & Shea, E. (1990). *Creative Therapy II: 52 More Exercises for Groups.* Sarasota, FL: Professional Resource Exchange.

Dossick, J., & Shea, E. (1995). *Creative Therapy III: 52 More Exercises for Groups.* Sarasota, FL: Professional Resource Exchange.

Khalsa, S. S. (1996). *Group Exercises for Enhancing Social Skills and Self-Esteem.* Sarasota, FL: Professional Resource Exchange.

Khalsa, S. S. (1999). *Group Exercises for Enhancing Social Skills and Self-Esteem* (Vol. 2). Sarasota, FL: Professional Resource Exchange.

Korb-Khalsa, K. L., Leutenberg, E. A., & Azok, S. D. (2001). *Life Management Skills I* (13th Ed.). Plainview, NY: Wellness Reproductions Publishing.

Korb-Khalsa, K. L., Leutenberg, E. A., & Azok, S. D. (2002). *Life Management Skills II* (10th Ed.). Plainview, NY: Wellness Reproductions Publishing.

Korb-Khalsa, K. L., Leutenberg, E. A., & Azok, S. D. (2001). *Life Management Skills III* (6th Ed.). Plainview, NY: Wellness Reproductions Publishing.

Korb-Khalsa, K. L., & Leutenberg, E. A. (1999). *Life Management Skills IV* (3rd Ed.). Beachwood, OH: Wellness Reproductions Publishing.

Korb-Khalsa, K. L., & Leutenberg, E. A. (2001). *Life Management Skills V* (3rd Ed.). Plainview, NY: Wellness Reproductions Publishing.

Korb-Khalsa, K. L., & Leutenberg, E. A. (2000). *Life Management Skills VI* (1st Ed.). Plainview, NY: Wellness Reproductions Publishing.

Korb-Khalsa, K. L., & Leutenberg, E. A. (2002). *Life Management Skills VII* (1st Ed.). Plainview, NY: Wellness Reproductions Publishing

Link, A. L. (1997). *Group Work with Elders: 50 Therapeutic Exercises for Reminiscence, Validation, and Remotivation.* Sarasota, FL: Professional Resource Exchange.

McKay, M., & Rogers, P. (2000). *The Anger Control Workbook.* Oakland, CA: New Harbinger Publications.

Napier, R. W., & Gershenfeld M. K. (1985). *Groups Theory and Experience* (3rd Ed.). Boston, MA: Houghton Mifflin.

Perkinson, R. R., (1997). *Chemical Dependency Counseling: A Practical Guide.* Thousand Oaks, CA: Sage Publications.

Williams, M. B., & Poijula, S. (2000). *The PTSD Workbook.* Oakland, CA: New Harbinger Publications.